The Best of the World's Classics

VOL. II

ROME

234 B.C.—180 A.D.

MARCUS AURELIUS

CÆSAR

CICERO

SENECA

THE BEST OF THE WORLD'S CLASSICS

RESTRICTED TO PROSE

HENRY CABOT LODGE
EDITOR-IN-CHIEF

FRANCIS W. HALSEY
ASSOCIATE EDITOR

With an Introduction, Biographical and Explanatory Notes, etc.

IN TEN VOLUMES

Vol. II
ROME

FUNK & WAGNALLS COMPANY
NEW YORK AND LONDON

Copyright, 1909, by
FUNK & WAGNALLS COMPANY
[Printed in the United States of America]

CONTENTS

Vol. II—Rome

	Page
CATO THE CENSOR—(Born in 234 B.C., died in 149.)	
Of Work on a Roman Farm. (From "De Re Rustica." Translated by Dr. E. Wilson)	3
CICERO—(Born in 106 B.C., assassinated in 43.)	
I The Blessings of Old Age. (From the "Cato Major." Translated by Cyrus R. Edmonds)	8
II On the Death of His Daughter Tullia. (A letter to Sulpicius)	34
III Of Brave and Elevated Spirits. (From Book I of the "Offices." Translated by Cyrus R. Edmonds)	37
IV Of Scipio's Death and of Friendship. From the "Dialog on Friendship." Translated by Cyrus R. Edmonds)	43
JULIUS CÆSAR—(Born in 100 B.C., assassinated in 44.)	
I The Building of the Bridge Across the Rhine. (From Book IV of the "Commentaries on the Gallic War." Translated by McDivett and W. S. Bohn)	61
II The Invasion of Britain. (From Book V of the "Commentaries on the Gallic War." Translated by McDivett and Bohn)	64

CONTENTS

	Page
III Overcoming the Nervii. (From Book II of the "Commentaries on the Gallic War." Translated by McDivett and Bohn)	71
IV The Battle of Pharsalia and the Death of Pompey. (From Book III of the "Commentaries on the Gallic War." Translated by McDivett and Bohn)	78

SALLUST—(Born about 86 B.C., died about 34.)

I The Genesis of Catiline. (From the "Conspiracy of Catiline." Translated by J. S. Watson)	91
II The Fate of the Conspirators. (From the "Conspiracy of Catiline." Translated by J. S. Watson)	98

LIVY—(Born in 59 B.C., died in 17 A.D.)

I Horatius Cocles at the Bridge. (From Book II of the "History of Rome." Translated by D. Spillan and Cyrus R. Edmonds)	105
II Hannibal's Crossing of the Alps. (From Book XXI of the "History of Rome." Translated by Spillan and Edmonds)	108
III Hannibal and Scipio at Zama. (From Book XXX of the "History of Rome." Translated by Spillan and Edmonds)	117

SENECA—(Born about 4 B.C., died in 65 A.D.)

I Of the Wise Man. (From Book II of the "Minor Essays." Translated by Aubrey Stewart)	128

CONTENTS

	Page
II Of Consolation for the Loss of Friends. (From Book VI of the "Minor Essays." Translated by Aubrey Stewart)	134
III To Nero on Clemency. (From the "Minor Essays." Translated by Aubrey Stewart)	141
IV The Pilot. (From Epistle 85. Translated by Thomas Lodge)	149
V Of a Happy Life. (From Book VII of the "Minor Essays." Translated by Aubrey Stewart)	153

PLINY THE ELDER—(Born in 23 A.D., perished in the Eruption of Vesuvius.)

I The Qualities of the Dog. (From the "Natural History." Translated by Bostock and Riley)	162
II Three Great Artists of Greece. (From the "Natural History." Translated by Bostock and Riley)	165

QUINTILIAN—(Born about 35 A.D., died about 95.)

The Orator Must Be a Good Man. (From Book XII, Chapter I, of the "Institutes." Translated by J. S. Watson)	171

TACITUS—(Born about 55 A.D., died about 117.)

I From Republican to Imperial Rome. (From Book I of the "Annals." The Oxford translation revised)	177
II The Funeral of Germanicus. (From Book III of the "Annals." The Oxford translation revised)	183

CONTENTS

	Page
III The Death of Seneca. (From Book XV of the "Annals." The Oxford translation revised)	189
IV The Burning of Rome by Order of Nero. (From Book XV of the "Annals." The Oxford translation revised)	193
V The Burning of the Capitol at Rome. (From Book III of the "History." The Oxford translation revised)	202
VI The Siege of Cremona. (From Book III of the "History." The Oxford translation revised)	205
VII Agricola. (The Oxford translation revised)	212

PLINY THE YOUNGER—(Born in 63 A.D., died in 113.)

I Of the Christians in His Province. (From the "Letters." The Melmoth translation revised)	218
II To Tacitus on the Eruption of Vesuvius. (From the "Letters." The Melmoth translation revised)	222

SUETONIUS—(Lived in the first half of the second century A.D.)

I The Last Days of Augustus. (From the "Lives of the Cæsars." Translated by Alexander Thomson, revised by Forester)	231
II The Good Deeds of Nero. (From the "Lives of the Cæsars." Translated by Thomson, revised by Forester)	236

CONTENTS

Page

III The Death of Nero. (From the "Lives of the Cæsars." Translated by Thomson, revised by Forester) . 241

MARCUS AURELIUS—(Born in 121 A.D., died in 180.)

His Debt to Others. (From the "Meditations." Translated by George Long) 248

ROME

234 B.C.—180 A.D.

CATO, THE CENSOR

Born in Tusculum, Italy, in 234 B.C., died in 149; celebrated as statesman, general, and writer; questor under Scipio in 204; Consul in 195; served in Spain in 194; censor in 184; ambassador to Carthage in 150; one of the chief instigators of the third Punic war; among his writings are "De Re Rustica" and "Origines."[1]

OF WORK ON A ROMAN FARM[2]

WHEN the owner of the farm and slaves visits his country villa, after saluting the household god, he should the same day, if possible, go round the farm; if not the same day, he should do so the day after. On seeing how the farm is being cultivated, and what work has been done or left undone, he should call for his steward and inquire for his account of what work has been done and what remains to be done. He should ask whether the work has been completed in good time and whether what is left uncompleted can be finished. He should find what wine has been made, and what wheat stored. When he has gone into these

---

[1] Cato was Rome's first thoroughly national author. He is usually classed as the creator of Latin prose. Other Roman authors of his time wrote in Greek. Cato bitterly opposed Greek learning, declaring that, when Greece should give Rome her literature, she would "corrupt everything." On Cato's mind no outside literary influence ever prevailed. He has been called "the most original writer that Rome ever produced."

[2] From "De Re Rustica." Translated for this work by Dr. Epiphanius Wilson.

particulars, he should ask for an account of the days spent in accomplishing the work.

If the work does not seem satisfactory and the steward should excuse himself by declaring that he has done his best, that the slaves were good for nothing, that the weather was bad, that some slaves had run away, that he himself had been called off on public service, and should allege other such excuses, he should still be strictly called to account. He should be asked if on rainy or tempestuous days he had seen that indoor operations had been carried on. Had the wine-casks been scoured and lined with pitch; had the house-cleaning been done; had the grain been taken from the thrashing-floor to the granary; had manure been thrown from the stables and cow-houses and piled into heaps; had the seed been winnowed; had any rope been made; had the old rope been repaired, and had he seen that the slaves mended their coats and caps. He should be reminded that on religious festivals old ditches might have been cleared out, the public road mended, briers cut down, the garden dug over, the meadow cleared, the trees trimmed, thorns pulled up by the roots, the grain ground and a general clearing up carried through. He should also be told that when slaves were sick their rations should be cut down.

When the matters have been settled to the master's satisfaction, he should take measures to see that what has not been done be at once accomplished. He should then proceed to consider the account of the farm, and a consideration of the amount of grain which has been prepared for fodder. He should have returns made of wine and olive-oil, and learn how much has been consumed, how much sold, how much is left over and may be put on sale. If there is a deficit any year, he should order it to be made up from the outside, and whatever is above the needs of the farm sold. If there is anything to let out on contract, he should order this to be done, and concerning the work which he wishes to be thus accomplished he should give his order in writing. As regards the cattle he should order them to be sold by auction, and in the same way should sell the oil, if the price of oil has risen; likewise the superfluous wine and corn of the estate. He should also order to be sold worn-out bulls, blemished cattle, blemished sheep, wool, hides, any plow that is old, old tools, old slaves, slaves who are diseased, or anything else which is useless, for the owner of a farm must be a seller and not a purchaser.

The owner of a farm and of slaves must begin to study in early manhood the cultivation and sowing of the land. He should, however, think a long time before building his villa, but not about farming his property, which he should set about at once. Let him wait until his thirty-sixth year and then build, provided his whole property is under cultivation. So build that neither the villa be disproportionately small in comparison with the farm nor the farm in comparison with the villa. It behooves a slave-owner to have a well-built country house, containing a wine-cellar, a place for storing olive-oil, and casks in such numbers that he may look forward with delight to a time of scarcity and high prices, and this will add not only to his wealth, but to his influence and reputation. He must have winepresses of the first order, that his wine may be well made. When the olives have been picked, let oil be at once made or it will turn out rancid. Recollect that every year the olives are shaken from the trees in great number by violent storms. If you gather them up quickly and have vessels ready to receive them, the storm will have done them no harm and the oil will be all the greener and better. If the olives be on the ground or even on the barn floor too long, the oil made from them will be fetid. Olive-oil will be always good and sweet if it be promptly made.

The following are the duties of a steward: He must maintain strict discipline, and see that the festivals are observed. While he keeps his hands off the property of a neighbor, let him look well to his own. The slaves are to be kept from quarreling. If any of them commits a fault, he should be punished in a kindly manner. The steward must see that the slaves are comfortable and suffer neither from cold nor hunger. By keeping them busy he will prevent them from running into mischief or stealing. If the steward sets his face against evil doing, evil will not be done by them. His master must call him to task if he let evil doing go unpunished. If one slave do him any service, he should show gratitude that the others may be encouraged to do right. The steward must not be a gadder or a diner-out, but must give all his attention to working the slaves, and considering how best to carry out his master's instructions. . . .

It is at times worth while to gain wealth by commerce, were it not so perilous; or by usury, were it equally honorable. Our ancestors, however, held, and fixt by law, that a thief should be condemned to restore double, a usurer quadruple. We thus see how much worse they thought it for a citizen to be a money-lender than a thief. Again, when they praised a good man, they praised him as a good farmer or a good husbandman. Men so praised were held to have received the highest praise. For myself, I think well of a merchant as a man of energy and studious of gain; but it is a career, as I have said, that leads to danger and ruin. However, farming makes the bravest men and the sturdiest soldiers, and of all sources of gain is the surest, the most natural, and the least invidious, and those who are busy with it have the fewest bad thoughts.[3]

[3] The translation of this paragraph is taken from Cruttwell's "History of Roman Literature."

CICERO

Born in 106 B.C., assassinated in 43; celebrated as orator, philosopher, statesman, and man of letters; served in the social war in 89; traveled in Greece and Asia in 79-77; questor in Sicily in 75; accused Verres in 70; prætor in 66; as Consul suppress Catiline's conspiracy in 63; banished in 58; recalled in 57; proconsul in Cicilia in 51-50; joined Pompey in 49; pronounced orations against Mark Antony in 44-43; proscribed by the Second Triumvirate in 43; of his orations fifty-seven are extant, with fragments of twenty others; other extant works include "De Oratore," "De Republica," "Cato Major," "De Officiis," and four collections of letters.

I

THE BLESSINGS OF OLD AGE[1]

Nor even now do I feel the want of the strength of a young man, no more than when a young man I felt the want of the strength of the bull or of the elephant. What one has, that one ought to use; and whatever you do, you should do it with all your strength. For what expression can be more contemptible than that of Milo[2] of Crotona, who, when he was now an old man, and was looking at the prize-fighters exercising themselves on the course, is reported to have looked at his

---

[1] From the "Cato Major, an Essay on Old Age." Translated by Cyrus R. Edmonds. This work is composed in the form of a dialog, in which, in the person of Cato the Censor as speaker, the benefits of old age are pointed out.

[2] A famous athlete who was many times crowned at the Pythian and Olympian games.

8

CICERO

arms, and, weeping over them, to have said, "But these, indeed, are now dead." Nay, foolish man, not these arms so much as yourself; for you never derived your nobility from yourself, but from your chest and your arms. Nothing of the kind did Sextus Ælius ever say, nothing of the kind many years before did Titus Coruncanius, nothing lately did Publius Crassus; by whom instructions in jurisprudence were given to their fellow citizens, and whose wisdom was progressive even to their latest breath. For the orator, I fear lest he be enfeebled by old age; for eloquence is a gift not of mind only, but also of lungs and strength. On the whole, that melodiousness in the voice is graceful, I know not how, even in old age; which, indeed, I have not lost, and you see my years.

Yet there is a graceful style of eloquence in an old man, unimpassioned and subdued, and very often the elegant and gentle discourse of an eloquent old man wins for itself a hearing; and if you have not yourself the power to produce this effect, yet you may be able to teach it to Scipio and Lælius. For what is more delightful than old age surrounded with the studious attention of youth? Shall we not leave even such a resource to old age, as to teach young men, instruct them, train them to every department of duty? an employment, indeed, than which what can be more noble? But, for my part, I thought the Cneius and Publius Scipios,[3] and your two grandfathers,

[3] Cneius Scipio was Consul in 222, and with Marcellus completed the conquest of Cisalpine Gaul. He served with his brother Publius Cicero against the Carthaginians in Spain, where, after several victories, both were slain in 212 B.C.

L. Æmilius and P. Africanus, quite happy in the attendance of noble youths; nor are any preceptors of liberal accomplishments to be deemed otherwise than happy, tho their strength hath fallen into old age and failed; altho that very failure of strength is more frequently caused by the follies of youth than by those of old age; for a lustful and intemperate youth transmits to old age an exhausted body. Cyrus too, in Xenophon, in that discourse which he delivered on his deathbed when he was a very old man, said that he never felt that his old age had become feebler than his youth had been. I recollect, when a boy, that Lucius Metellus,[4] who, when four years after his second consulship he had been made "pontifex maximus," and for twenty-two years held that sacerdotal office, enjoyed such good strength at the latter period of his life, that he felt no want of youth. There is no need for me to speak about myself, and yet that is the privilege of old age, and conceded to my time of life.

Do you see how, in Homer, Nestor very often proclaims his own virtues? for he was now living in the third generation of men; nor had he occasion to fear lest, when stating the truth about himself, he should appear either too arrogant or too talkative; for, as Homer says, from his tongue speech flowed sweeter than honey; for which charm he stood in need of no strength of body; and yet the famous chief of Greece nowhere wishes to have ten men like Ajax, but like Nestor; and he does not doubt if that should happen, Troy would in a short time perish.

[4] Lucius Metellus, a Roman general who defeated the Carthaginians at Panormus, now Palermo, Sicily, in 250 B.C.

But I return to myself. I am in my eighty-fourth year. In truth I should like to be able to make the same boast that Cyrus did; but one thing I can say, that altho I have not, to be sure, that strength which I had either as a soldier in the Punic war or as questor in the same war, or as Consul in Spain, or, four years afterward, when as military tribune I fought a battle at Thermopylæ, in the consulship of Marcus Acilius Glabrio; yet, as you see, old age has not quite enfeebled me or broken me down: the senate-house does not miss my strength, nor the rostra, nor my friends, nor my clients, nor my guests; for I have never agreed to that old and much-praised proverb which advises you to become an old man early if you wish to be an old man long. I for my part would rather be an old man for a shorter length of time than be an old man before I was one. And, therefore, no one as yet has wished to have an interview with me to whom I have been denied as engaged.

But I have less strength than either of you two. Neither even do you possess the strength of Titus Pontius the centurion; is he, therefore, the more excellent man? Only let there be a moderate degree of strength, and let every man exert himself as much as he can; and in truth that man will not be absorbed in regretting the want of strength. Milo, at Olympia, is said to have gone over the course while supporting on his shoulders a live ox. Whether, then, would you rather have this strength of body, or Pythagoras' strength of intellect, bestowed upon you? In a word, enjoy that blessing while you have it; when it is gone, do not lament it, unless, indeed, young men ought to lament the loss of boyhood, and those a little advanced in age the loss of adolescence. There is a definite career in life, and one way of nature, and that a simple one; and to every part of life its own peculiar period has been assigned; so that both the feebleness of boys, and the high spirit of young men, and the steadiness of now fixt manhood, and the maturity of old age, have something natural which ought to be enjoyed in their own time. I suppose that you hear, Scipio, what your grandfather's host, Masinissa,[5] is doing at this day, at the age of ninety. When he has commenced a journey on foot, he never mounts at all; when on horseback, he never dismounts; by no rain, by no cold, is he prevailed upon to have his head covered; that there is in him the greatest hardiness of frame; and therefore he performs all the duties and functions of a king. Exercise, therefore, and temperance, even in old age, can preserve some remnant of our pristine vigor.

Is there no strength in old age? neither is strength exacted from old age. Therefore, by our laws and institutions, our time of life is relieved from those tasks which can not be supported without strength. Accordingly, so far are we from being compelled to do what we can not do that we are not even compelled to do as much as we can. But so feeble are many old men that they can not execute any task of duty or any function of life whatever; but that in truth is not the peculiar fault of old age, but belongs in common to bad health. How feeble was the son

[5] Masinissa, king of a small territory in northern Africa, was at first an ally of Carthage against Rome, but afterward became an ally of Rome against Carthage.

of Publius Africanus, he who adopted you! What feeble health, or rather no health at all, had he! and had that not been so, he would have been the second luminary of the state; for to his paternal greatness of soul a richer store of learning had been added. What wonder, therefore, in old men, if they are sometimes weak when even young men can not escape that.

We must make a stand, Scipio and Lælius, against old age, and its faults must be atoned for by activity; we must fight, as it were, against disease, and in like manner against old age. Regard must be paid to health; moderate exercises must be adopted; so much of meat and drink must be taken that the strength may be recruited, not opprest. Nor, indeed, must the body alone be supported, but the mind and the soul much more; for these also, unless you drop oil on them as on a lamp, are extinguished by old age. And our bodies, indeed, by weariness and exercise, become opprest; but our minds are rendered buoyant by exercise. For as to those of whom Cæcilius speaks, "foolish old men," fit characters for comedy, by these he denotes the credulous, the forgetful, the dissolute, which are the faults not of old age, but of inactive, indolent, drowsy old age. As petulance and lust belong to the young more than to the old, yet not to all young men, but to those who are not virtuous; so that senile folly, which is commonly called dotage, belongs to weak old men, and not to all. Four stout sons, five daughters, so great a family, and such numerous dependents, did Appius manage, altho both old and blind; for he kept his mind intent like a bow, nor did he languidly sink under the weight of old age. He retained not only authority, but also command, over his family; the slaves feared him; the children respected him; all held him dear; there prevailed in that house the manners and good discipline of our fathers. For on this condition is old age honored if it maintains itself, if it keeps up its own right, if it is subservient to no one, if even to its last breath it exercises control over its dependents. For, as I like a young man in whom there is something of the old, so I like an old man in whom there is something of the young; and he who follows this maxim, in body will possibly be an old man, but he will never be an old man in mind.

I have in hand my seventh book of Antiquities; I am collecting all the materials of our early history; of all the famous causes which I have defended; I am now completing the pleadings;[6] I am employed on the law of augurs, of pontiffs, of citizens. I am much engaged also in Greek literature, and, after the manner of the Pythagoreans, for the purpose of exercising my memory, I call to mind in the evening what I have said, heard, and done on each day. These are the exercises of the understanding; these are the racecourses of the mind; while I am perspiring and toiling over these, I do not greatly miss my strength of body. I attend my friends, I come into the senate very often, and spontaneously bring forward things much and long thought of,

---

[6] The translator explains that the speeches here referred to, as collected and published by Cato, numbered about 150. Cato was known to his contemporaries as "the Roman Demosthenes." Later writers often referred to him as "Cato the orator."

and I maintain them by strength of mind, not of body; and if I were unable to perform these duties, yet my couch would afford me amusement, when reflecting on those matters which I was no longer able to do, but that I am able is owing to my past life; for, by a person who always lives in these pursuits and labors, it is not perceived when old age steals on. Thus gradually and unconsciously life declines into old age; nor is its thread suddenly broken, but the vital principle is consumed by length of time.

Then follows the third topic of blame against old age, that they say it has no pleasures. Oh, noble privilege of age! if indeed it takes from us that which is in youth the greatest defect. For listen, most excellent young men, to the ancient speech of Archytas[7] of Tarentum, a man eminently great and illustrious, which was reported to me when I, a young man, was at Tarentum with Quintus Maximus. He said that no more deadly plague than the pleasure of the body was inflicted on men by nature; for the passions, greedy of that pleasure, were in a rash and unbridled manner incited to possess it; that hence arose treasons against one's country, hence the ruining of states, hence clandestine conferences with enemies — in short, that there was no crime, no wicked act, to

---

[7] Archytas was a Greek philosopher, eminent also as statesman, mathematician, and general. He lived about 400 B.C., and is credited with having saved the life of Plato through his influence with Dionysius, the tyrant of Syracuse. He was seven times general of the army of Tarentum and successful in all his campaigns; eminent also for domestic virtues. He is pronounced by a writer in Smith's "Dictionary" to have been "among the very greatest men of antiquity." He was drowned while making a voyage in the Adriatic.

the undertaking of which the lust of pleasure did not impel; but that fornications and adulteries and every such crime were provoked by no other allurements than those of pleasure. And whereas either nature or some god had given to man nothing more excellent than his mind, that to this divine function and gift, nothing was so hostile as pleasure; since where lust bore sway, there was no room for self-restraint; and in the realm of pleasure, virtue could by no possibility exist. And that this might be the better understood, he begged you to imagine in your mind any one actuated by the greatest pleasure of the body that could be enjoyed; he believed no one would doubt but that so long as the person was in that state of delight, he would be able to consider nothing in his mind, to attain nothing by reason, nothing by reflection; wherefore that there was nothing so detestable and so destructive as pleasure, inasmuch as that when it was excessive and very prolonged, it extinguished all the light of the soul.

Nearchus of Tarentum, our host, who had remained throughout in friendship with the Roman people, said he had heard from older men that Archytas held this conversation with Caius Pontius the Samnite, the father of him by whom, in the Caudian [a] battle, Spurius Postumius and Titus Veturius, the consuls, were overcome, on which occasion Plato the Athenian had been present at that discourse; and I find that he came to Tarentum in the consulship of Lucius Camillus and

[a] Caudium was a Samnite town near which the Romans were defeated by Pontius Herennius.

Appius Claudius.[9] Wherefore do I adduce this? that we may understand that if we could not by reason and wisdom despise pleasure, great gratitude would be due to old age for bringing it to pass that that should not be a matter of pleasure which is not a matter of duty. For pleasure is hostile to reason, hinders deliberation, and, so to speak, closes the eyes of the mind, nor does it hold any intercourse with virtue. I indeed acted reluctantly in expelling from the senate Lucius Flaminius, brother of that very brave man Titus Flaminius,[10] seven years after he had been Consul; but I thought that his licentiousness should be stigmatized. For that man, when he was Consul in Gaul, was prevailed on at a banquet by a courtezan to behead one of those who were in chains, condemned on a capital charge. He escaped in the censorship of his brother Titus, who had immediately preceded me; but so profligate and abandoned an act of lust could by no means be allowed to pass by me and Flaccus, since with private infamy it combined the disgrace of the empire.

I have often heard from my elders, who said that, in like manner, they, when boys, had heard from old men, that Caius Fabricius was wont to wonder that when he was ambassador to King Pyrrhus, he had heard from Cineas the Thessa-

[9] Not the Appius Claudius from whom the Appian Way and one of the great aqueducts were named. The older Appius Claudius, here referred to, lived in the century that followed Plato.

[10] Titus Flaminius, general and statesman, was Consul in 198 B.C. It was not Titus, but Caius Flaminius, who built the famous circus and road bearing his name. Caius lived at an earlier period.

lian that there was a certain person at Athens who profest himself a wise man, and that he was accustomed to say that all things which we did were to be referred to pleasure; and that hearing him say so, Manius Curius and Titus Coruncanius were accustomed to wish that that might be the persuasion of the Samnites and Pyrrhus[11] himself, that they might the more easily be conquered when they had given themselves up to pleasure. Manius Curius had lived with Publius Decius, who, five years before the consulship of the former, had devoted himself for the commonwealth in his fourth consulship. Fabricius had been acquainted with him, and Coruncanius had also known him, who, as well from his own conduct in life, as from the great action of him whom I mention, Publius Decius, judged that there was doubtless something in its own nature excellent and glorious, which should be followed for its own sake, and which, scorning and despising pleasure, all the worthiest men pursued. . . .

But why do I refer to others? Let me now return to myself. First of all, I always had associates in clubs; and clubs were established when I was questor, on the Idæan worship of the great mother being adopted. Therefore I feasted with my associates altogether in a moderate way, but there was a kind of fervor peculiar to that time of life, and as that advances, all things will become every day more subdued. For I did not calculate the gratification of those banquets by the pleasures of the body so much as by the meet-

[11] Pyrrhus, king of Epirus, the eminent military genius, who several times defeated the Romans before he was finally overthrown by them at Beneventum in 275 B.C.

ings of friends and conversations. For well did our ancestors style the reclining of friends at an entertainment, because it carried with it a union of life, by the name "convivium" better than the Greeks do, who call this same thing as well by the name of "compotatio" as "concœnatio"; so that what in that kind (of pleasures) is of the least value that they appear most to approve of.

For my part, on account of the pleasure of conversation, I am delighted also with seasonable entertainments, not only with those of my own age, of whom very few survive, but with those of your age, and with you; and I give great thanks to old age, which has increased my desire for conversation, and taken away that of eating and drinking. But even if such things delight any person (that I may not appear altogether to have declared war against pleasure, of which perhaps a certain limited degree is even natural), I am not aware that even in these pleasures themselves old age is without enjoyment. For my part, the presidencies established by our ancestors delight me; and that conversation, which after the manner of our ancestors, is kept up over our cups from the top of the table; and the cups, as in the Symposium of Xenophon, small and dewy, and the cooling of the wine in summer, and in turn either the sun, or the fire in winter—practises which I am accustomed to follow among the Sabines also—and I daily join a party of neighbors, which we prolong with various conversation till late at night, as far as we can. But there is not, as it were, so ticklish a sensibility of pleasures in old men. I believe it; but then neither is there the desire. However, nothing is irksome unless you long for it. Well did Sophocles, when a certain man inquired of him advanced in age whether he enjoyed venereal pleasures, reply, "The gods give me something better; nay, I have run away from them with gladness, as from a wild and furious tyrant." For to men fond of such things, it is perhaps disagreeable and irksome to be without them; but to the contented and satisfied it is more delightful to want them than to enjoy them; and yet he does not want who feels no desire; therefore I say that this freedom from desire is more delightful than enjoyment.

But if the prime of life has more cheerful enjoyment of those very pleasures, in the first place they are but petty objects which it enjoys, as I have said before; then they are those of which old age, if it does not abundantly possess them, is not altogether destitute. As he is more delighted with Turpio Ambivius, who is spectator on the foremost bench, yet he also is delighted who is in the hindmost; so youth having a close view of pleasures is perhaps more gratified; but old age is as much delighted as is necessary in viewing them at a distance. However, of what high value are the following circumstances, that the soul, after it has served out, as it were, its time under lust, ambition, contention, enmities, and all the passions, shall retire within itself, and, as the phrase is, live with itself? But if it has, as it were, food for study and learning, nothing is more delightful than an old age of leisure. I saw Caius Gallus, the intimate friend of your father, Scipio, almost expiring in the employment of calculating the sky and the earth. How often did daylight overtake him when he had begun to draw some figure by night, how often did night, when he had begun in the morning! How it did delight him to predict to us the eclipses of the sun and the moon, long before their occurrence! What shall we say in the case of pursuits less dignified, yet, notwithstanding, requiring acuteness! How Nævius did delight in his Punic war! how Plautus in his Truculentus! how in his Pseudolus! I saw also the old man Livy,[12] who, tho he had brought a play upon the stage six years before I was born, in the consulship of Cento and Tuditanus, yet advanced in age even to the time of my youth. Why should I speak of Publius Licinius Crassus' study both of pontifical and civil law? or of the present Publius Scipio, who within these few days was created chief pontiff? Yet we have seen all these persons whom I have mentioned, ardent in these pursuits when old men. But as to Marcus Cethegus, whom Ennius rightly called the "marrow of persuasion," with what great zeal did we see him engage in the practise of oratory, even when an old man! What pleasures, therefore, arising from banquets, or plays, or harlots, are to be compared with these pleasures? And these, indeed, are the pursuits of learning, which too, with the sensible and well educated, increase along with their age; so that is a noble saying of Solon, when he says in a certain verse, as I observed before, that he grew old learning many things every day—than which pleasure of the mind, certainly, none can be greater.

I come now to the pleasures of husbandmen, with which I am excessively delighted, which are not checked by any old age, and appear in my

[12] Livius Andronicus, who lived in Rome about 240 B.C.

mind to make the nearest approach to the life of a wise man. For they have relation to the earth, which never refuses command, and never returns without interest that which it hath received; but sometimes with less, generally with very great interest. And yet for my part it is not only the product, but the virtue and nature of the earth itself that delight me, which, when in its softened and subdued bosom it has received the scattered seed, first of all confines what is hidden within it, from which harrowing, which produces that effect, derives its name (*occatio*); then, when it is warmed by heat and its own compression, it spreads it out, and elicits from it the verdant blade, which, supported by the fibers of the roots, gradually grows up, and, rising on a jointed stalk, is now enclosed in a sheath, as if it were of tender age, out of which, when it hath shot up, it then pours forth the fruit of the ear, piled in due order, and is guarded by a rampart of beards against the pecking of the smaller birds. Why should I, in the case of vines, tell of the plantings, the risings, the stages of growth? That you may know the repose and amusement of my old age, I assure you that I can never have enough of that gratification. For I pass over the peculiar nature of all things which are produced from the earth; which generates such great trunks and branches from so small a grain of the fig or from the grape-stone, or from the minutest seeds of other fruits and roots; shoots, plants, twigs, quicksets, layers, do not these produce the effect of delighting any one even to admiration? The vine, indeed, which by nature is prone to fall, and is borne down to the ground, unless it be propt, in order to raise itself up, embraces with its tendrils, as it were with hands, whatever it meets with, which, as it creeps with manifold and wandering course, the skill of the husbandmen pruning with the knife, restrains from running into a forest of twigs, and spreading too far in all directions.

Accordingly, in the beginning of spring, in those twigs which are left, there rises up as it were at the joints of the branches that which is called a bud, from which the nascent grape shows itself, which, increasing in size by the moisture of the earth and the heat of the sun, is at first very acid to the taste, and then as it ripens grows sweet, and being clothed with its large leaves does not want moderate warmth, and yet keeps off the excessive heat of the sun; than which what can be in fruit on the one hand more rich, or on the other hand more beautiful in appearance? Of which not only the advantage, as I said before, but also the cultivation and the nature itself delight me; the rows of props, the joining of the heads, the tying up and propagation of vines, and the pruning of some twigs, and the grafting of others, which I have mentioned. Why should I allude to irrigations, why to the diggings of the ground, why to the trenching by which the ground is made much more productive? Why should I speak of the advantage of manuring? I have treated of it in that book which I wrote respecting rural affairs, concerning which the learned Hesiod has not said a single word, tho he has written about the cultivation of the land. But Homer, who, as appears to me, lived many ages before, introduces Lærtes soothing the regret which he felt for his son by tilling the land and manuring it. Nor indeed is rural life delightful by reason of corn-fields only and meadows and vineyards and groves, but also for its gardens and orchards; also for the feeding of cattle, the swarms of bees, and the variety of all kinds of flowers. Nor do plantings only give me delight, but also graftings, than which agriculture has invented nothing more ingenious. . . .

Was then their old age to be pitied who amused themselves in the cultivation of land? In my opinion, indeed, I know not whether any other can be more happy; and not only in the discharge of duty, because to the whole race of mankind the cultivation of the land is beneficial; but also from the amusement, which I have mentioned, and that fulness and abundance of all things which are connected with the food of men, and also with the worship of the gods; so that, since some have a desire for these things, we may again put ourselves on good terms with pleasure. For the wine-cellar of a good and diligent master is always well stored; the oil-casks, the pantry also, the whole farmhouse is richly supplied; it abounds in pigs, kids, lambs, hens, milk, cheese, honey. Then, too, the countrymen themselves call the garden a second dessert. And then what gives a greater relish to these things is that kind of leisure labor, fowling and hunting. Why should I speak of the greenness of meadows, or the rows of trees, or the handsome appearance of vineyards and olive grounds? Let me cut the matter short. Nothing can be either more rich in use or more elegant in appearance than ground well tilled, to the enjoyment of which old age is so far from being an obstacle that it is even an invitation and allurement. For where can that age be better warmed either by basking in the sun or by the fire, or again be more healthfully refreshed by shades or waters? Let the young, therefore, keep to themselves their arms, horses, spears, clubs, tennisball, swimmings, and races; to us old men let them leave out of many amusements the *tali* and *tesseræ;* and even in that matter it may be as they please, since old age can be happy without these amusements. . . .

What, therefore, should I fear if after death I am sure either not to be miserable or to be happy? Altho who is so foolish, even if young, as to be assured that he will live even till the evening? Nay, that period of life has many more probabilities of death that ours has; young men more readily fall into diseases, suffer more severely, are cured with more difficulty, and therefore few arrive at old age. Did not this happen so we should live better and more wisely, for intelligence, and reflection, and judgment reside in old men, and if there had been none of them, no states could exist at all. But I return to the imminence of death. What charge is that against old age, since you see it to be common to youth also? I experienced not only in the case of my own excellent son, but also in that of your brothers, Scipio, men plainly marked out for the highest distinction, that death was common to every period of life. Yet a young man hopes that he will live a long time, which expectation an old man can not entertain. His hope is but a foolish one; for what can be more foolish than to regard uncertainties as certainties, delusions as truths? An old man indeed has nothing to hope for; yet he is

in so much the happier state than a young one;
since he has already attained what the other is
only hoping for. The one is wishing to live long,
the other has lived long.

And yet, good gods! what is there in man's life
that can be called long? For allow the latest period; let us anticipate the age of the kings of
Tartessii. For there dwelt, as I find it recorded,
a man named Arganthonius at Gades;[13] who
reigned for eighty years, and lived 120. But to
my mind, nothing whatever seems of long duration to which there is any end. For when that
arrives, then the time which has passed has flown
away; that only remains which you have secured
by virtue and right conduct. Hours indeed depart
from us, and days and months and years; nor
does past time ever return, nor can it be discovered what is to follow. Whatever time is assigned
to each to live, with that he ought to be content;
for neither need the drama be performed entire
by the actor in order to give satisfaction, provided
he be approved in whatever act he may be; nor
need the wise man live till the *plaudite*. For the
short period of life is long enough for living well
and honorably; and if you should advance further, you need no more grieve than farmers do
when the loveliness of spring-time hath passed,
that summer and autumn have come. For spring
represents the time of youth, and gives promise
of the future fruits; the remaining seasons are

---

[13] A small island (now a peninsula), lying off the coast of
Spain. It is to-day called Cadiz, but anciently was known as
Erythia, Tartessus, and Gades. It was founded about 1100
B.C., by the Phenicians, of whose western commerce it was
the center.

CICERO

intended for plucking and gathering in those fruits. Now the harvest of old age, as I have often said, is the recollection and abundance of blessings previously secured. In truth everything that happens agreeably to nature is to be reckoned among blessings. What, however, is so agreeable to nature as for an old man to die? which even is the lot of the young, tho nature opposes and resists. And thus it is that young men seem to me to die just as when the violence of flame is extinguished by a flood of water; whereas old men die, as the exhausted fire goes out, spontaneously, without the exertion of any force; and as fruits when they are green are plucked by force from the trees, but when ripe and mellow drop off, so violence takes away their lives from youths, maturity from old men—a state which to me indeed is so delightful that the nearer I approach to death, I seem, as it were, to be getting sight of land, and at length, after a long voyage, to be just coming into harbor.

Of all the periods of life there is a definite limit; but of old age there is no limit fixt; and life goes on very well in it, so long as you are able to follow up and attend to the duty of your situation, and, at the same time, to care nothing about death; whence it happens that old age is even of higher spirit and bolder than youth. Agreeable to this was the answer given to Pisistratus,[14] the tyrant, by Solon, when on the former inquiring, "in reliance on what hope he so boldly withstood him," the latter is said to have answered, "on old age." The happiest end of life is this—when the

[14] The tyrant of Athens who reigned thirty-three years and died about 527 B.C.

mind and the other senses being unimpaired, the same nature which put it together takes asunder her own work. As in the case of a ship or a house, he who built them takes them down most easily; so the same nature which has compacted man most easily breaks him up. Besides, every fastening of glue, when fresh, is with difficulty torn asunder, but easily when tried by time. Hence it is that that short remnant of life should be neither greedily coveted nor without reason given up; and Pythagoras forbids us to abandon the station or post of life without the orders of our commander, that is, of God.[15] There is indeed a saying of the wise Solon in which he declares that he does not wish his own death to be unattended by the grief and lamentation of friends. He wishes, I suppose, that he should be dear to his friends. But I know not whether Ennius does not say with more propriety,

"Let no one pay me honor with tears, nor celebrate my funeral with mourning."

He conceives that a death ought not to be lamented which immortality follows. Besides, a dying man may have some degree of consciousness, but that for a short time, especially in the case of an old man; after death, indeed, consciousness either does not exist or it is a thing to be desired. But this ought to be a subject of study from our youth to be indifferent about death, without which study

[15] Melmoth has commented on this passage that, altho suicide too generally prevailed among the Greeks and Romans, the wisest philosophers condemned it. "Nothing," he says, "can be more clear and explicit" than the prohibition imposed by Pythagoras, Socrates, and Plato.

CICERO

no one can be of tranquil mind. For die we certainly must, and it is uncertain whether or not on this very day. He, therefore, who at all hours dreads impending death, how can he be at peace in his mind? concerning which there seems to be no need of such long discussion, when I call to mind not only Lucius Brutus, who was slain in liberating his country; nor the two Decii, who spurred on their steeds to a voluntary death; nor Marcus Atilius,[16] who set out to execution that he might keep a promise pledged to the enemy; nor the two Scipios, who even with their very bodies sought to obstruct the march of the Carthaginians; nor your grandfather Lucius Paulus,[17] who by his death atoned for the temerity of his colleague in the disgraceful defeat at Cannæ; nor Marcus Marcellus,[18] whose corpse not even the most merciless foe suffered to go without the honor of sepulture; but that our legions, as I have remarked in my Antiquities, have often gone with cheerful and undaunted mind to that place from which they believed that they should never return. Shall, then, well-instructed old men be afraid of that which young men, and they not only ignorant, but mere peasants, despise? On the whole, as it seems to me indeed, a satiety of all pursuits causes a satiety of life. There are pursuits pecul-

---

[16] Better known as the famous Regulus, whose alleged speech to the "Conscript Fathers" has been declaimed by generations of schoolboys.

[17] Lucius Paulus died at the battle of Cannæ, which was precipitated by his colleague Terentius Varro in 260 B.C., 40,000 Romans being killed by the Carthaginians.

[18] Marcellus, a Roman consul, who fought against Hannibal and was killed in an ambuscade.

iar to boyhood; do therefore young men regret the loss of them? There are also some of early youth; does settled age, which is called middle life, seek after these? There are also some of this period; neither are they looked for by old age. There are some final pursuits of old age; accordingly, as the pursuits of the earlier parts of life fall into disuse, so also do those of old age; and when this has taken place, satiety of life brings on the seasonable period of death.

Indeed, I do not see why I should not venture to tell you what I myself think concerning death; because I fancy I see it so much the more clearly in proportion as I am less distant from it. I am persuaded that your fathers, Publius Scipio and Caius Lælius, men of the greatest eminence and very dear friends of mine, are living, and that life too which alone deserves the name of life. For while we are shut up in this prison of the body, we are fulfilling, as it were, the function and painful task of destiny; for the heaven-born soul has been degraded from its dwelling-place above, and, as it were, buried in the earth, a situation uncongenial to its divine and immortal nature. But I believe that the immortal gods have shed souls into human bodies, that beings might exist who might tend the earth, and by contemplating the order of the heavenly bodies might imitate it in the manner and regularity of their lives. Nor have reason and argument alone influenced me thus to believe, but likewise the high name and authority of the greatest philosophers. I used to hear that Pythagoras and the Pythagoreans, who were all but our neighbors, who were formerly called the Italian philosophers, had no doubt that we possess souls derived from the universal divine mind. Moreover, tne arguments were conclusive to me which Socrates delivered on the last day of his life concerning the immortality of the soul—he who was pronounced by the oracle of Apollo the wisest of all men. But why say more? I have thus persuaded myself, such is my belief; that since such is the activity of our souls, so tenacious their memory of things past and their sagacity regarding things future, so many arts, so many sciences, so many discoveries, that the nature which comprizes these qualities can not be mortal; and since the mind is ever in action and has no source of motion, because it moves itself, I believe that it never will find any end of motion, because it never will part from itself; and that since the nature of the soul is uncompounded, and has not in itself any admixture heterogeneous and dissimilar to itself, I maintain that it can not undergo dissolution; and if this be not possible, it can not perish; and it is a strong argument that men know very many things before they are born, since when mere boys, while they are learning difficult subjects, they so quickly catch up numberless ideas, that they seem not to be learning them then for the first time, but to remember them, and to be calling them to recollection. Thus did our Plato argue. . . .

Let me, if you please, revert to my own views. No one will ever persuade me that either your father, Paulus, or two grandfathers, Paulus and Africanus, or the father of Africanus, or his uncle, or the many distinguished men whom it is unnecessary to recount, aimed at such great exploits as might reach to the recollection of posterity had they not perceived in their mind that posterity belonged to them. Do you suppose, to boast a little of myself, after the manner of old men, that I should have undergone such great toils, by day and night, at home and in service, had I thought to limit my glory by the same bounds as my life? Would it not have been far better to pass an easy and quiet life without any toil or struggle? But I know not how my soul, stretching upward, has ever looked forward to posterity, as if, when it had departed from life, then at last it would begin to live. And, indeed, unless this were the case, that souls were immortal, the souls of the noblest of men would not aspire above all things to an immortality of glory.

Why need I adduce that the wisest man ever dies with the greatest equanimity, the most foolish with the least? Does it not seem to you that the soul, which sees more and further, sees that it is passing to a better state, while that body whose vision is duller, does not see it? I, indeed, am transported with eagerness to see your fathers, whom I have respected and loved; nor in truth is it those only I desire to meet whom I myself have known; but those also of whom I have heard or read, and have myself written. Whither, indeed, as I proceed, no one assuredly should easily force me back, nor, as they did with Pelias, cook me again to youth. For if any god should grant me that from this period of life I should become a child again and cry in the cradle, I should earnestly refuse it; nor in truth should I like, after having run, as it were, my course, to be called back to the starting-place from the goal. For what comfort has life? What trouble has it not, rather? But grant that it has; yet it assuredly has either satiety or limitation (of its pleasures). For I am not disposed to lament the loss of life, which many men, and those learned men too, have often done; neither do I regret that I have lived, since I have lived in such a way that I conceive I was not born in vain; and from this life I depart as from a temporary lodging, not as from a home.

For nature has assigned it to us as an inn to sojourn in, not a place of habitation. Oh, glorious day! when I shall depart to that divine company and assemblage of spirits, and quit this troubled and polluted scene. For I shall go not only to those great men of whom I have spoken before, but also to my son Cato, than whom never was better man born, nor more distinguished for pious affection, whose body was burned by me, whereas, on the contrary, it was fitting that mine should be burned by him. But his soul not deserting me, but oft looking back, no doubt departed to those regions whither it saw that I myself was destined to come. This, tho a distress to me, I seemed patiently to endure; not that I bore it with indifference, but I comforted myself with the recollection that the separation and distance between us would not continue long. For these reasons, O Scipio (since you said that you with Lælius were accustomed to wonder at this), old age is tolerable to me, and not only not irksome, but even delightful. And if I am wrong in this, that I believe the souls of men to be immortal, I willingly delude myself; nor do I desire that this mistake, in which I take pleasure, should be wrested from me as long as I live; but if I, when dead, shall have no consciousness, as some narrow-minded philosophers imagine, I do not fear lest dead philosophers should ridicule this my delusion. But if we are not destined to be immortal, yet it is a desirable thing for a man to expire at his fit time. For, as nature prescribes a boundary to all other things, so does she also to life. Now old age is the consummation of life, just as of a play, from the fatigue of which we ought to escape, especially when satiety is superadded. This is what I had to say on the subject of old age, to which may you arrive! that, after having experienced the truth of those statements which you have heard from me, you may be enabled to give them your approbation.

II

ON THE DEATH OF HIS DAUGHTER
TULLIA [19]

YES, my dear Servius, I could indeed wish you had been with me, as you say, at the time of my terrible trial. How much it was in your power to help me if you had been here, by sympathizing with, and I may almost say, sharing equally in

[19] Cicero's daughter was born about 79 B.C., and thrice married, the last time to Dolabella, who has been described as "one of the most profligate men of a profligate age." She was divorced from Dolabella in 44 B.C., gave birth to a son soon afterward, and died in the same year. Cicero's letter was written in reply to one which he had received from Servius Sulpicius, a celebrated Roman jurist. Cicero intended to erect a temple as a memorial to Tullia, but the death of Cæsar and the unsettled state of public affairs that ensued, and in which Cicero was concerned, prevented him from doing so.

my grief, I readily perceive from the fact that after reading your letter I now feel myself considerably more composed; for not only was all that you wrote just what is best calculated to soothe affliction, but you yourself in comforting me showed that you too had no little pain at heart. Your son Servius, however, has made it clear, by every kindly attention which such an occasion would permit of, both how great his respect was for myself and also how much pleasure his kind feeling for me was likely to give you; and you may be sure that, while such attentions from him have often been more pleasant to me, they have never made me more grateful.

It is not, however, only your arguments and your equal share—I may almost call it—in this affliction which comforts me, but also your authority; because I hold it shame in me not to be bearing my trouble in a way that you, a man endowed with such wisdom, think it ought to be borne. But at times I feel broken down, and I scarcely make any struggle against my grief, because those consolations fail me which under similar calamities were never wanting to any of those other people whom I put before myself as models for imitation. Both Fabius Maximus, for example, when he lost a son who had held the consulship, the hero of many a famous exploit; and Lucius Paulus, from whom two were taken in one week; and your own kinsman Gallus; and Marcus Cato, who was deprived of a son of the rarest talents and the rarest virtue—all these lived in times when their individual affliction was capable of finding a solace in the distinctions they used to earn from their country.

For me, however, after being stript of all those distinctions which you yourself recall to me, and which I had won for myself by unparalleled exertions, only that one solace remained which has been torn away. My thoughts were not diverted by work for my friends, or by the administration of affairs of state; there was no pleasure in pleading in the courts; I could not bear the very sight of the Senate House; I felt, as was indeed too true, that I had lost all the harvest of both my industry and my success. But whenever I wanted to recollect that all this was shared with you and other friends I could name, and whenever I was breaking myself in and forcing my spirit to bear these things with patience, I always had a refuge to go to where I might find peace, and in whose words of comfort and sweet society I could rid me of all my pains and griefs. Whereas now, under this terrible blow, even those old wounds which seemed to have healed up are bleeding afresh; for it is impossible for me now to find such a refuge from my sorrows at home in the business of the state as in those days I did in that consolation of home, which was always in store whenever I came away sad from thoughts of state to seek for peace in her happiness. And so I stay away both from home and from public life; because home now is no more able to make up for the sorrow I feel when I think of our country than our country is for my sorrow at home. I am therefore looking forward all the more eagerly to your coming, and long to see you as early as may possibly be; no greater alleviation can be offered me than a meeting between us for friendly intercourse and conversation. I hope, however, that your return is to take place, as I hear it is, very shortly. As for myself, while there are abundant reasons for wanting to see you as soon as possible, my principal one is in order that we may discuss together beforehand the best method of conduct for present circumstances, which must entirely be adapted to the wishes of one man only, a man nevertheless who is far-seeing and generous, and also, as I think I have thoroughly ascertained, to me not at all ill-disposed and to you extremely friendly. But admitting this, it is still a matter for much deliberation what is the line—I do not say of action, but of keeping quiet—that we ought by his good leave and favor to adopt. Farewell!

III

OF BRAVE AND ELEVATED SPIRITS [20]

A SPIRIT altogether brave and elevated is chiefly discernible by two characters. The first consists in a low estimate of mere outward circumstances, since it is convinced that a man ought to admire, desire, or court nothing but what is virtuous and becoming; and that he ought to succumb to no man, nor to any perturbation either of spirit or fortune. The other thing is that, possest of such a spirit as I have just mentioned, you should perform actions which are great and of the greatest utility, but extremely arduous, full of difficulties

[20] From Book I of the "Offices." Translated by Cyrus R. Edmonds.

and danger both to life and the many things which pertain to life.

In the latter of those two characters consist all the glory, the majesty, and, I add, the utility; but the causes and the efficient means that form great men is in the former, which contains the principles that elevate the soul, and gives it a contempt for temporary considerations. Now, this very excellence consists in two particulars: you are to deem that only to be good is to be virtuous, and that you be free from all mental irregularity. For we are to look upon it as the character of a noble and an elevated soul, to slight all those considerations that the generality of mankind account great and glorious, and to despise them, upon firm and durable principles; while strength of mind and greatness of resolution are discerned in bearing those calamities which, in the course of man's life, are many and various, so as not to be driven from your natural disposition, nor from the dignity of a wise man; for it is not consistent that he who is not subdued by fear should be subjugated by passion, nor that he who has shown himself invincible by toil should be conquered by pleasure. Wherefore, we ought to watch and avoid the love of money; for nothing so truly characterizes a narrow, groveling disposition as to love riches; and nothing is more noble and more exalted than to despise riches if you have them not, and if you have them, to employ them in beneficence and liberality.

An inordinate passion for glory, as I have already observed, is likewise to be guarded against; for it deprives us of liberty, the only prize for which men of elevated sentiments ought to con-

CICERO

tend. Power is so far from being desirable in itself that it sometimes ought to be refused, and sometimes to be resigned. We should likewise be free from all disorders of the mind, from all violent passion and fear, as well as languor, voluptuousness, and anger, that we may possess that tranquillity and security which confer alike consistency and dignity. Now, many there are, and have been, who, courting that tranquillity which I have mentioned here, have withdrawn themselves from public affairs and taken refuge in retirement. Among these, some of the noblest and most prominent of our philosophers; and some persons, of strict and grave dispositions, were unable to bear with the manners either of the people or their rulers; and some have lived in the country, amusing themselves with the management of their private affairs. Their aim was the same as that of the powerful, that they might enjoy their liberty, without wanting anything or obeying any person; for the essence of liberty is to live just as you please. . . .

But, since most persons are of opinion that the achievements of war are more glorious than civil affairs, this judgment needs to be restricted; for many, as generally is the case with high minds and enterprising spirits, especially if they are adapted to military life and are fond of warlike achievements, have often sought opportunities of war from their fondness for glory; but if we are willing to judge truly, many are the civil employments of greater importance, and of more renown, than the military.

For tho Themistocles is justly praised — his name is now more illustrious than that of Solon, and his glorious victory at Salamis is mentioned preferably to the policy of Solon, by which he first confirmed the power of the Areopagus—the one should not be considered more illustrious than the other; for the one availed his country only for once—the other is lastingly advantageous; because by it the laws of the Athenians, and the institutions of their ancestors, are preserved. Now, Themistocles could not have stated any respect in which he benefited the Areopagus, but Solon might with truth declare that Themistocles had been advantaged by him; for the war was carried on by the counsels of that senate which was constituted by Solon.

We may make the same observation with regard to Pausanias [21] and Lysander among the Lacedæmonians; for all the addition of empire which their conquests are supposed to have brought to their country is not to be compared to the laws and economy of Lycurgus; for indeed, owing to these very causes they had armies more subordinate and courageous. In my eyes, Marcus Scaurus (who flourished when I was but a boy) was not inferior to Caius Marius; [22] nor, after I came to have a concern in the government, Quintus Catulus [23] to Cneius Pompey. An army abroad is but of small service, unless there be a wise adminis-

[21] Pausanias, a Spartan general, was the son of Cloembrotus, the king of Sparta, killed at the battle of Leuctra. Pausanias commanded at Platæa; but having conducted a treasonable correspondence with Xerxes, was starved to death as a punishment.

[22] The general who contended against Sulla in the Civil war.

[23] Catulus was consul with Marius in 102 B.C. He acted with Sulla during the Civil war.

CICERO

tration at home. Nor did that good man and great general Africanus perform a more important service to his country when he razed Numantia than did that private citizen P. Nasica,[24] when at the same period he killed Tiberius Gracchus. An action which it is true was not merely of a civil nature; for it approaches to a military character, as being the result of force and courage; but it was an action performed without an army, and from political considerations. . . .

Now all that excellence which springs from a lofty and noble nature is altogether produced by the mental and not by the corporeal powers. Meanwhile, the body ought to be kept in such action and order as that it may be always ready to obey the dictates of reason and wisdom, in carrying them into execution, and in persevering under hardships. But with regard to that *honestas* we are treating of, it consists wholly in the thoughtful application of the mind, by which the civilians who preside over public affairs are equally serviceable to their country as they who wage wars. For it often happens that by such counsels wars are either not entered into or they are brought to a termination; sometimes they are even undertaken, as the third Punic war was by the advice of Marcus Cato, whose authority was powerful, even after he was dead.

[24] Nasica, "a fierce and stiff-necked aristocrat," was of the family of Scipios. When the consuls refused to resort to violence against Tiberius Gracchus, it was he who led the senators forth from their meeting-place against the popular assembly outside, with whom ensued a fight, in which Gracchus was killed by a blow from a club. Nasica left Rome soon after, seeking safety. After spending some time as a wandering exile, he died at Pergamus.

Wisdom in determining is therefore preferable to courage in fighting; but in this we are to take care that we are not swayed by an aversion to fighting rather than by a consideration of expediency. Now in engaging in war we ought to make it appear that we have no other view than peace. But the character of a brave and resolute man is not to be ruffled with adversity, and not to be in such confusion as to quit his post, as we say, but to preserve a presence of mind, and the exercise of reason, without departing from his purpose. And while this is the characteristic of a lofty spirit, so this also is that of a powerful intellect; namely, to anticipate futurity in thought, and to conclude beforehand what may happen on either side, and, upon that, what measures to pursue, and never be surprized so as to say, "I had not thought of that." Such are the operations of a genius, capacious and elevated; of such a one as relies on its own prudence and counsel; but to rush precipitately into the field, and to encounter an enemy with mere physical force has somewhat in it that is barbarous and brutal. When the occasion, however, and its necessity compel it, we should resist with force, and prefer death to slavery or dishonor.

CICERO

IV

OF SCIPIO'S DEATH AND OF FRIENDSHIP[25]

SHOULD I say that I am not distrest by the loss of Scipio, philosophers may determine with what propriety I should do so; but assuredly I should be guilty of falsehood. For I am distrest at being bereaved of such a friend, as no one, I consider, will ever be to me again, and, as I can confidently assert, no one ever was; but I am not destitute of a remedy. I comfort myself, and especially with this consolation, that I am free from that error by which most men, on the decease of friends, are wont to be tormented; for I feel that no evil has happened to Scipio; it has befallen myself, if indeed it has happened to any. Now to be above measure distrest at one's own troubles is characteristic of the man who loves not his friend, but himself. In truth, as far as he is concerned, who

[25] From the Dialogue on "Friendship." Translated by Cyrus R. Edmonds. Lælius, a Roman who was contemporary with the younger Scipio, is made the speaker in the passage here quoted. Lælius, was a son of Caius Lælius, the friend and companion of the elder Scipio, whose actions are so interwoven with those of Scipio that a writer in Smith's "Dictionary" says, "It is difficult to relate them separately." The younger Lælius was intimate with the younger Scipio in a degree almost as remarkable as his father had been with the elder. The younger, immortalized by Cicero's treatise on Friendship, was born about 186 B.C., and was a man of fine culture noted as an orator. His personal worth was so generally esteemed that it survived to Seneca's day. One of Seneca's injunctions to a friend was that he should "live like Lælius."

can deny that his end was glorious? for unless he had chosen to wish for immortality, of which he had not the slightest thought, what did he fail to obtain which it was lawful for a man to wish for? A man who, as soon as he grew up, by his transcendent merit far surpassed those sanguine hopes of his countrymen which they had conceived regarding him when a mere boy, who never stood for the consulship, yet was made Consul twice; on the first occasion, before his time; on the second, at the proper age as regarded himself, tho for the commonwealth almost too late; who, by overthrowing two cities,[26] most hostile to our empire, put an end not only to all present but all future wars. What shall I say of his most engaging manners; of his dutiful conduct to his mother; his generosity to his sisters; his kindness to his friends; his uprightness toward all? These are known to you; and how dear he was to the state was displayed by its mourning at his death. . . .

The authority of the ancients has more weight with me, either that of our own ancestors, who paid such sacred honors to the dead, which surely they would not have done if they thought those honors did in no way affect them, or that of those who once lived in this country, and enlightened, by their institutions and instructions, Magna Græcia[27] (which now indeed is entirely destroyed, but

[26] Scipio Africanus minor by whom Carthage was destroyed in 146 B.C., and Numantia, a town of Spain, was destroyed in 133 B.C. From the letter he obtained the surname of Numantinus.

[27] Magna Græcia was a name given by the ancients to that part of southern Italy which, before the rise of the Roman state, was colonized by Greeks. Its time of greatest splendor

then was flourishing), or of him who was pronounced by the oracle of Apollo to be the wisest of men, who did not say first one thing and then another, as is generally done, but always the same; namely, that the souls of men are divine, and that when they have departed from the body, a return to heaven is opened to them, and the speediest to the most virtuous and just. This same opinion was also held by Scipio; for he indeed, a very few days before his death, as if he had a presentiment of it, when Philus and Manilius were present, and many others, and you also, Scævola, had gone with me, for three days descanted on the subject of government; of which discussion the last was almost entirely on the immortality of souls, which he said he had learned in sleep through a vision from Africanus. If this be the fact, that the spirit of the best man most easily flies away in death, as from the prison-house and chains of the body, whose passage to the gods can we conceive to have been readier than that of Scipio? Wherefore, to be afflicted at this his departure, I fear, would be the part rather of an envious person than of a friend. . . .

But yet I so enjoy the recollection of our friendship that I seem to have lived happily because I lived with Scipio, with whom I had a common anxiety on public and private affairs, and with whom my life both at home and abroad was associated, and there existed that, wherein

was the seventh and sixth centuries B.C.; that is, intermediate between the Homeric age and the Periclean. Among its leading cities were Cumæ, Sybaris, Locri, Regium, Tarentum, Heraclea, and Pæstum. At the last-named place imposing ruins still survive.

consists the entire strength of friendship, an entire agreement of inclinations, pursuits, and sentiments. That character for wisdom, therefore, which Fannius a little while ago mentioned does not so delight me, especially since it is undeserved, as the hope that the recollection of our friendship will last forever. And it is the more gratifying to me because scarcely in the history of the world are three or four pairs of friends mentioned by name; and I indulge in the hope that the friendship of Scipio and Lælius will be remembered. . . .

I can only urge you to prefer friendship to all human possessions; for there is nothing so suited to our nature, so well adapted to prosperity or adversity. But first of all, I am of opinion that except among the virtuous friendship can not exist; I do not analyze this principle too closely, as they do who inquire with too great nicety into those things, perhaps with truth on their side, but with little general advantage; for they maintain that there is no good man but the wise man. Be it so, yet they define wisdom to be such as no mortal has ever attained to; whereas we ought to contemplate those things which exist in practise and in common life, and not the subjects of fictions or of our own wishes. I would never pretend to say that Caius Fabricius, Marius Curius, and Titus Coruncanius, whom our ancestors esteemed wise, were wise according to the standard of these moralists. Wherefore let them keep to themselves the name of wisdom, both invidious and unintelligible, and let them allow that these were good men—nay, they will not even do that; they will declare that this can not be granted except to a wise man.

CICERO

Let us therefore proceed with our dull genius, as they say. Those who so conduct themselves and so live that their honor, their integrity, their justice, and liberality are approved; so that there is not in them any covetousness, or licentiousness, or boldness; and that they are of great consistency, as those men whom I have mentioned above—let us consider these worthy of the appellation of good men, as they have been accounted such, because they follow (as far as men are able) nature, which is the best guide of a good life. For I seem to myself to have this view, that we are so formed by nature that there should be a certain social tie among all; stronger, however, as each approaches nearer us. Accordingly, citizens are preferable to foreigners, and relatives to strangers; for with the last-named, Nature herself has created a friendly feeling, tho this has not sufficient strength. For in this respect friendship is superior to relationship, because from relationship benevolence can be withdrawn and from friendship it can not; for with the withdrawal of benevolence the very name of friendship is done away, while that of relationship remains. Now how great the power of friendship is may be best gathered from this consideration, that out of the boundless society of the human race, which Nature herself has joined together, friendship is a matter so contracted, and brought into so narrow a compass, that the whole of affection is confined to two, or at any rate to very few.

Now friendship is nothing else than a complete union of feeling on all subjects, divine and human, accompanied by kindly feeling and attachment, than which, indeed, I am not aware whether, with the exception of wisdom, anything better has been bestowed on man by the immortal gods. Some men prefer riches, others good health, others influence, others again honors, many prefer even pleasures; the last, indeed, is the characteristic of beasts; while the former are fleeting and uncertain, depending not so much on our own purpose as on the fickleness of fortune. Whereas those who place the supreme good in virtue, therein do admirably; but this very virtue itself both begets and constitutes friendship; nor without this virtue can friendship exist at all. Now let us define this virtue according to the usage of life and of our common language; and let us not measure it, as certain learned persons do, by pomp of language; and let us include among the good those who are so accounted—the Paulli, the Catos, the Galli, the Scipios, and the Phili; with these men ordinary life is content; and let us pass over those who are nowhere found to exist. Among men of this kind, therefore, friendship finds facilities so great that I can scarcely describe them.

In the first place—to whom can life be "worth living," as Ennius says, who does not repose on the mutual kind feeling of some friend? What can be more delightful than to have one to whom you can speak on all subjects just as to yourself? Where would be the great enjoyment in prosperity if you had not one to rejoice in it equally with yourself? And adversity would indeed be difficult to endure without some one who would bear it even with greater regret than yourself. In short, all other objects that are sought after are severally suited to some one single purpose—riches, that you may spend them; power that you may be courted; honors, that you may be extolled; pleasures, that you may enjoy them; good health, that you may be exempt from harm, and perform the functions of the body. Whereas friendship comprizes the greatest number of objects possible; wherever you turn yourself, it is at hand; shut out of no place, never out of season, never irksome; and therefore we do not use fire and water, as they say, on more occasions than we do friendship. And I am not now speaking of commonplace or ordinary friendship (tho even that brings delight and benefit), but of real and true friendship, such as belonged to those of whom very few are recorded; for prosperity, friendship renders more brilliant, and adversity more supportable, by dividing and communicating it.

And while friendship embraces very many and great advantages, she undoubtedly surpasses all in this, that she shines with a brilliant hope over the future, and never suffers the spirit to be weakened or to sink. Besides, he who looks on a true friend looks, as it were, upon a kind of image of himself; wherefore friends, tho absent, are still present; tho in poverty, they are rich; tho weak, yet in the enjoyment of health; and, what is still more difficult to assert, tho dead they are alive; so entirely does the honor, the memory, the regret of friends attend them; from which circumstance the death of the one seems to be happy, and the life of the other praiseworthy; nay, should you remove from nature the cement of kind feelings, neither a house nor a city will be able to stand; even the cultivation of the land will not continue. If it be not clearly perceived how great is the power of friendship and concord, it can be distinctly inferred from quarrels and dissensions; for what house is there so established, or what state so firmly settled, that may not utterly be overthrown by hatred and dissension? From which it may be determined how much advantage there is in friendship. They relate, indeed, that a certain learned man of Agrigentum [28] promulgated in Greek verses the doctrine that all things which cohere throughout the whole world, and all things that are the subjects of motion, are brought together by friendship, and are dispelled by discord; and this principle all men understand, and illustrate by their conduct. Therefore, if at any time any act of a friend has been exhibited, either in undergoing or in sharing dangers, who is there that does not extol such an act with the highest praise? . . .

Now if such be the influence of integrity, that we love it even in those whom we have never seen, and, what is much more, even in an enemy, what wonder if men's feelings are affected when they seem to discover the goodness and virtue of those with whom they may become connected by intercourse? altho love is confirmed by the reception of kindness, and by the discovery of an earnest sympathy, and by close familiarity, which things being added to the first emotion of the mind and the affections, there is kindled a large amount of kindly feeling. And if any

[28] Empedocles, philosopher, poet, and historian, who lived at Agrigentum in Sicily, about 490-430 B.C., and wrote a poem on the doctrines of Pythagoras. A legend has survived that he jumped into the crater of Etna, in order that people might conclude, from his complete disappearance, that he was a god. Matthew Arnold's poem on this incident is among his better-known works.

imagine that this proceeds from a sense of weakness, so that there shall be secured a friend, by whom a man may obtain that which he wants, they leave to friendship a mean and, indeed, if I may so speak, anything but respectable origin, when they make her to be born of indigence and want; were this the case, then in proportion as a man judged that there were the least resources in himself, precisely in that degree would he be best qualified for friendship, whereas the fact is far otherwise. For just as a man has most confidence in himself, and as he is most completely fortified by worth and wisdom, so that he needs no one's assistance, and feels that all his resources reside in himself, in the same proportion he is most highly distinguished for seeking out and forming friendships. For what did Africanus want of me? Nothing whatever, nor indeed did I need aught from him; but I loved him from admiration of his excellence; he in turn perhaps was attached to me from some high opinion which he entertained of my character, and association fostered our affection. But altho many and great advantages ensued, yet it was not from any hope of these that the causes of our attachment sprang; for as we are beneficent and liberal not to exact favor in return (for we are not usurers in kind actions), but by nature are inclined to liberality, thus I think that friendship is to be desired, not attracted by the hope of reward, but because the whole of its profit consists in love only. From such opinions, they who, after the fashion of beasts, refer everything to pleasure, widely differ, and no great wonder, since they can not look up to anything lofty, magnificent, or divine who cast all their thoughts on an object so mean and contemptible.

Therefore let us exclude such persons altogether from our discourse; and let us ourselves hold this opinion, that the sentiment of loving and the attachment of kind feelings are produced by nature when the evidence of virtue has been established; and they who have eagerly sought the last-named draw nigh and attach themselves to it, that they may enjoy the friendship and character of the individual they have begun to love, and that they may be commensurate and equal in affection, and more inclined to confer a favor than to claim any return. And let this honorable struggle be maintained between them; so not only will the greatest advantages be derived from friendship, but its origin from nature rather than from a sense of weakness will be at once more impressive and more true. For if it were expediency that cemented friendships, the same when changed would dissolve them; but because nature can never change, therefore true friendships are eternal. . . .

Listen, then, my excellent friends, to the discussion which was very frequently held by me and Scipio on the subject of friendship; altho he indeed used to say that nothing was more difficult than that friendship should continue to the end of life; for it often happened either that the same course was not expedient to both parties or that they held different views of politics; he remarked also that the characters of men often changed, in some cases by adversity, in others

CICERO

by old age becoming oppressive; and he derived an authority for such notions from a comparison with early life, because the strongest attachments of boys are constantly laid aside with the prætexta; even if they should maintain it to manhood, yet sometimes it is broken off by rivalry, for a dowried wife, or some other advantage which they can not both attain. And even if men should be carried on still further in their friendship, yet that feeling is often undermined should they fall into rivalry for preferments; for there is no greater enemy to friendship than covetousness of money, in most men, and even in the best, an emulous desire of high offices and glory, in consequence of which the most bitter enmities have often arisen between the dearest friends. For great dissensions, and those in most instances justifiable, arise when some request is made of friends which is improper, as, for instance, that they should become either the ministers of their lust or their supporters in the perpetration of wrong; and they who refuse to do so, it matters not however virtuously, yet are accused of discarding the claims of friendship by those persons whom they are unwilling to oblige; but they who dare to ask anything of a friend, by their very request seem to imply that they would do anything for the sake of that friend; by the complaining of such persons, not only are long-established intimacies put an end to, but endless animosities are engendered. All these many causes, like so many fatalities, are ever threatening friendship, so that, he said, to escape them all seemed to him a proof not merely of wisdom, but even of good fortune. . . .

Let this, therefore, be established as a primary law concerning friendship, that we expect from our friends only what is honorable, and for our friends' sake do what is honorable; that we should not wait till we are asked; that zeal be ever ready, and reluctance far from us; but that we take pleasure in freely giving our advice; that in our friendship, the influence of our friends, when they give good advice, should have great weight; and that this be employed to admonish not only candidly, but even severely, if the case shall require, and that we give heed to it when so employed; for, as to certain persons whom I understand to have been esteemed wise men in Greece, I am of opinion that some strange notions were entertained by them; but there is nothing which they do not follow up with too great subtlety; among the rest, that excessive friendships should be avoided, lest it should be necessary for one to feel anxiety for many; that every one has enough, and more than enough, of his own affairs; that to be needlessly implicated in those of other people is vexatious; that it was most convenient to hold the reins of friendship as loose as possible, so as either to tighten or slacken them when you please; for they argue that the main point toward a happy life is freedom from care, which the mind can not enjoy if one man be, as it were, in travail for others.

Nay, they tell us that some are accustomed to declare, still more unfeelingly (a topic which I have briefly touched upon just above), that friendships should be cultivated for the purpose of protection and assistance, and not for kind feeling or affection; and therefore the less a man possesses of independence and of strength, in the same degree he most earnestly desires friendships; that thence it arises that women seek the support of friendship more than men, and the poor more than the rich, and persons in distress rather than those who are considered prosperous. Admirable philosophy! for they seem to take away the sun from the world who withdraw friendship from life; for we receive nothing better from the immortal gods, nothing more delightful; for what is this freedom from care?—in appearances, indeed, flattering; but, in many cases, in reality to be disdained. Nor is it reasonable to undertake any honorable matter or action lest you should be anxious, or to lay it aside when undertaken; for if we fly from care, we must fly from virtue also; for it is impossible that she can, without some degree of distress, feel contempt and detestation for qualities opposed to herself; just as kind-heartedness for malice, temperance for profligacy, and bravery for cowardice. Accordingly, you see that upright men are most distrest by unjust actions; the brave with the cowardly; the virtuous with the profligate; and, therefore, this is the characteristic of a well-regulated mind, both to be well pleased with what is excellent and to be distrest with what is contrary. Wherefore, if trouble of mind befall a wise man (and assuredly it will, unless we suppose that all humanity is extirpated from his mind), what reason is there why we should altogether remove friendship from life, lest because of it we should take upon ourselves some troubles? for what difference is there (setting the emotions of the mind aside), I do not say between a man and a beast, but between a man and a stone, or log, or anything of that kind? For they do not deserve to be listened to who would have virtue to be callous and made of iron, as it were, which indeed is, as in other matters, so in friendship also, tender and susceptible; so that friends are loosened, as it were, by happy events, and drawn together by distresses.

Wherefore the anxiety which has often to be felt for a friend is not of such force that it should remove friendship from the world, any more than that the virtues, because they bring with them certain cares and troubles, should therefore be discarded. For when it produces friendship (as I said above), should any indication of virtue shine forth, to which a congenial mind may attach and unite itself—when this happens, affection must necessarily arise. For what is so unmeaning as to take delight in many vain things, such as preferments, glory, magnificent buildings, clothing and adornment of the body, and not to take an extreme delight in a soul endued with virtue, in such a soul as can either love or (so to speak) love in return? for there is nothing more delightful than the repayment of kindness and the interchange of devotedness and good offices. Now if we add this, which may with propriety be added, that nothing so allures and draws any object to itself as congeniality does friendship, it will of course be admitted as true that the good must love the good, and unite them to themselves, just as if connected by relationship and nature; for nothing is more apt to seek and seize on its like than nature. Wherefore this certainly is clear, Fannius and Scævola (in my opinion), that among the good a liking for the good is, as it were, inevitable; and this indeed is appointed by Nature herself as the very fountain of friendship.

But the same kind disposition belongs also to the multitude; for virtue is not inhuman, or cruel, or haughty, since she is accustomed to protect even whole nations, and to adopt the best measures for their welfare, which assuredly she would not do did she shrink from the affection of the vulgar. And to myself, indeed, those who form friendships with a view to advantage seem to do away with its most endearing bond; for it is not so much the advantage obtained through a friend as the mere love of that friend which delights; and then only what has proceeded from a friend becomes delightful if it has proceeded from zealous affection; and that friendship should be cultivated from a sense of necessity is so far from being the case that those who, being endowed with power and wealth, and especially with virtue (in which is the strongest support of friendship), have least need of another, are most liberal and generous. Yet I am not sure whether it is requisite that friends should never stand in any need; for wherein would any devotedness of mine to him have been exerted if Scipio had never stood in need of my advice or assistance at home or abroad? Wherefore friendship has not followed upon advantage, but advantage on friendship.

Persons, therefore, who are wallowing in indulgence will not need to be listened to if ever they shall descant upon friendship, which they have known neither by experience nor by theory. For who is there, by the faith of gods and men, who would desire, on the condition of his loving no one, and himself being loved by none, to roll in affluence, and live in a superfluity of all things? For this is the life of tyrants, in which undoubtedly there can be no confidence, no affection, no steady dependence on attachment; all is perpetually mistrust and disquietude—there is no room for friendship. For who can love either him whom he fears or him by whom he thinks he himself is feared? Yet are they courted, solely in hypocrisy, for a time; because, if perchance (as it frequently happens) they have been brought low, then it is perceived how destitute they were of friends. And this, they say, Tarquin[29] exprest; that when going into exile, he found out whom he had as faithful friends, and whom unfaithful ones, since then he could no longer show gratitude to either party; altho I wonder that, with such haughtiness and impatience of temper, he could find one at all. And as the character of the individual whom I have mentioned could not obtain true friends, so the riches of many men of rank exclude all faithful friendship; for not only is fortune blind herself, but she commonly renders blind those whom she embraces. . . .

He who, therefore, shall have shown himself in both cases, as regards friendship, worthy,

[29] Tarquinius Superbus, seventh and last King of Rome, occupied the throne for twenty-five years, and as a consequence of the rape of Lucretia by his son Sextus was banished about 509 B.C.

consistent, and stedfast; such a one we ought to esteem of a class of persons extremely rare— nay, almost godlike. Now, the foundation of that stedfastness and constancy, which we seek in friendship, is sincerity. For nothing is stedfast which is insincere. Besides, it is right that one should be chosen who is frank and good-natured, and congenial in his sentiments; one, in fact, who is influenced by the same motives, all of which qualities have a tendency to create sincerity. For it is impossible for a wily and tortuous disposition to be sincere. Nor in truth can the man who has no sympathy from nature, and who is not moved by the same considerations, be either attached or steady. To the same requisites must be added that he shall neither take delight in bringing forward charges nor believe them when they arise, all of which causes belong to that consistent principle of which now for some time I have been treating. Thus the remark is true which I made at first that friendship can exist only among the good; for it is the part of a good man (whom at the same time we may call a wise man) to observe these two rules in friendship: first, that there shall be nothing pretended or simulated (for even to hate openly better becomes the ingenuous man than by his looks to conceal his sentiments); in the next place, that not only does he repel charges when brought (against his friends) by any one, but is not himself suspicious, ever fancying that some infidelity has been committed by his friend. To all this there should be added a certain suavity of conversation and manners, affording, as it does, no inconsiderable zest to friendship. Now solemnity and gravity on all occasions, certainly, carry with them dignity; but friendship ought to be easier and more free and more pleasant, and tending more to every kind of politeness and good nature. . . .

JULIUS CÆSAR

Born in 100 B.C.; assassinated in 44; famous as general, statesman, orator, and writer; served in Mitylene in 80; captured by pirates in 76; questor in 68; pontifex maximus in 63; propretor in Spain in 61; member of the First Triumvirate in 60; Consul in 59; defeated the Helvetii in 58; invaded Britain in 55 and 54; crossed the Rhine in 55; crossed the Rubicon and began the Civil war in 49; dictator from 49 to 45; defeated Pompey in 48; reformed the calendar in 46; refused the diadem in 44; assassinated in the senate house in 44.[1]

I

THE BUILDING OF THE BRIDGE ACROSS THE RHINE[2]

CÆSAR, for those reasons which I have mentioned, had resolved to cross the Rhine; but to cross by ships he neither deemed to be sufficiently safe nor considered consistent with his own dignity or that of the Roman people. Therefore, altho the greatest difficulty in forming a bridge was presented to him, on account of the breadth, rapidity, and depth of the river, he nevertheless

---

[1] Cicero, whose praise of Cæsar as a writer has been shared by many readers since his time, described Cæsar's works as "unadorned, straightforward, and elegant, their ornament being stript off as it were a garment." Cæsar did his work so well that "he has deterred all men of sound taste from touching him."

[2] From Book IV of the "Commentaries on the Gallic War." Translated by McDivett and W. S. Bohn. The site of this bridge is believed to be in the neighborhood of Cologne.

considered that it ought to be attempted by him, or that his army ought not otherwise to be led over. He devised this plan of a bridge: he joined together, at the distance of two feet, two piles, each a foot and half thick, sharpened a little at the lower end, and proportioned in length to the depth of the river.

After he had, by means of engines, sunk these into the river, and fixt them at the bottom, and then driven them in with rammers, not quite perpendicularly, like a stake, but bending forward and sloping, so as to incline in the direction of the current of the river; he also placed two [other piles] opposite to these, at the distance of forty feet lower down, fastened together in the same manner, but directed against the force and current of the river. Both these, moreover, were kept firmly apart by beams two feet thick (the space which the binding of the piles occupied), laid in at their extremities between two braces on each side; and in consequence of these being in different directions and fastened on sides the one opposite to the other, so great was the strength of the work, and such the arrangement of the materials, that in proportion as the greater body of water dashed against the bridge, so much the closer were its parts held fastened together. These beams were bound together by timber laid over them in the direction of the length of the bridge, and were [then] covered with laths and hurdles; and, in addition to this, piles were driven into the water obliquely, at the lower side of the bridge, and these serving as buttresses, and being connected with every portion of the work, sustained the force of

JULIUS CÆSAR

the stream; and there were others also above the bridge, at a moderate distance, that if trunks of trees or vessels were floated down the river by the barbarians for the purpose of destroying the work, the violence of such things might be diminished by these defenses, and might not injure the bridge.

Within ten days after the timber began to be collected, the whole work was completed, and the whole army led over. Cæsar, leaving a strong guard at each end of the bridge, hastens into the territories of the Sigambri. In the mean time, ambassadors from several nations come to him, whom, on their suing for peace and alliance, he answers in a courteous manner, and orders hostages to be brought to him. But the Sigambri, at the very time the bridge was begun to be built, made preparations for a flight (by the advice of such of the Tenchtheri and Usipĕtes as they had among them), and quitted their territories and conveyed away all their possessions, and concealed themselves in deserts and woods.

Cæsar, having remained in their territories a few days, and burned all their villages and houses, and cut down their corn, proceeded into the territories of the Ubii; and having promised them his assistance, if they were ever harassed by the Suevi,[3] he learned from them these particulars: that the Suevi, after they had by means of their scouts found that the bridge was being built, had called a council, according to

[3] The Suevi were migratory Germans who, in Cæsar's time, occupied the eastern banks of the Rhine in and about the present country of Baden.

their custom, and sent orders to all parts of their state to remove from the towns and convey their children, wives, and all their possessions into the woods, and that all who could bear arms should assemble in one place; that the place thus chosen was nearly the center of those regions which the Suevi possest; that in this spot they had resolved to await the arrival of the Romans, and give them battle there. When Cæsar discovered this, having already accomplished all these things on account of which he had resolved to lead his army over—namely, to strike fear into the Germans, take vengeance on the Sigambri, and free the Ubii from the invasion of the Suevi, having spent altogether eighteen days beyond the Rhine, and thinking he had advanced far enough to serve both honor and interest—he returned into Gaul, and cut down the bridge.

II

THE INVASION OF BRITAIN[4]

THE interior portion of Britain is inhabited by those of whom they say that it is handed down by tradition that they were born in the island itself; the maritime portion by those who had passed over from the country of the Belgæ[5] for the purpose of plunder and making war; almost

[4] From Book V of the "Commentaries on the Gallic War."

[5] The Belgæ comprised various tribes that lived between the Seine and the Rhine and were the most warlike of the Gauls.

JULIUS CÆSAR

all of whom are called by the names of those states from which being sprung they went thither, and having waged war, continued there and began to cultivate the lands. The number of the people is countless, and their buildings exceedingly numerous, for the most part very like those of the Gauls; the number of cattle is great. They use either brass or iron rings, determined at a certain weight, as their money. Tin is produced in the midland regions; in the maritime, iron; but the quantity of it is small; they employ brass, which is imported. There, as in Gaul, is timber of every description, except beech and fir. They do not regard it lawful to eat the hare and the cock and the goose; they, however, breed them for amusement and pleasure. The climate is more temperate than in Gaul, the cold being less severe.

The island is triangular in its form, and one of its sides is opposite to Gaul. One angle of this side, which is in Kent, whither almost all ships from Gaul are directed, [looks] to the east; the lower looks to the south. This side extends about 500 miles. Another side lies toward Spain,[6] and the west, on which part is Ireland, less, as is reckoned, than Britain, by one half; but the passage [from it] into Britain is of equal distance with that from Gaul. In the middle of this voyage is an island which is called Mona;[7] many smaller islands besides are supposed to lie [there], of which islands some have written that at the time of the winter solstice it is night

[6] Cæsar's error re has often been commented on, Spain lying to the south, ather than to the west, of Britain.

[7] Now known as the Isle of Man.

there for thirty consecutive days. We, in our inquiries about that matter, ascertained nothing, except that, by accurate measurements with water, we perceived the nights to be shorter there than on the continent. The length of this side, as their account states, is 700 miles. The third side is toward the north, to which portion of the island no land is opposite; but an angle of that side looks principally toward Germany. This side is considered to be 800 miles in length. Thus the whole island is [about] 2,000 miles in circumference.

The most civilized of all these nations are they who inhabit Kent, which is entirely a maritime district, nor do their customs differ much from Gallic. Most of the inland inhabitants do not sow corn, but live on milk and flesh, and are clad with skins. All the Britans, indeed, dye themselves with wood, which occasions a bluish color, and thereby have a more terrible appearance in fight. They wear their hair long, and have every part of their body shaved except their head and upper lip. Ten and even twelve have wives common to them, and particularly brothers among brothers, and parents among their children; but if there be any issue by these wives, they are reputed to be the children of those by whom respectively each was first espoused when a virgin.

The horse and charioteers of the enemy contended vigorously in a skirmish with our cavalry on the march; yet so that our men were conquerors in all parts, and drove them to their woods and hills; but, having slain a great many, they pursued too eagerly, and lost some of their

JULIUS CÆSAR

men. However, the enemy, after some time had elapsed, when our men were off their guard, and occupied in the fortification of the camp, rushed out of the woods, and making an attack upon those who were placed on duty before the camp, fought in a determined manner; and two cohorts being sent by Cæsar to their relief, and these severally the first of two legions, when these had taken up their position at a very small distance from each other, as our men were disconcerted by the unusual mode of battle, the enemy broke through the middle of them most courageously, and retreated thence in safety. That day, Q. Laberius Durus, a tribune of the soldiers, was slain. The enemy, since more cohorts were sent against them, were repulsed.

In the whole of this method of fighting since the engagement took place under the eyes of all and before the camp, it was perceived that our men, on account of the weight of their arms, inasmuch as they could neither pursue [the enemy when] retreating, nor dare quit their standards, were little suited to this kind of enemy; that the horse also fought with great danger, because they [the Britons] generally retreated even designedly, and, when they had drawn off our men a short distance from the legions, leapt from their chariots and fought on foot in unequal [and to them advantageous] battle. But the system of cavalry engagement is wont to produce equal danger, and indeed the same, both to those who retreat and those who pursue. To this was added, that they never fought in close order, but in small parties and at great distances, and had detachments placed [in different parts], and then the one relieved the other, and the vigorous and fresh succeeded the wearied.

The following day the enemy halted on the hills, a distance from our camp, and presented themselves in small parties, and began to challenge our horse to battle with less spirit than the day before. But at noon, when Cæsar had sent three legions, and all the cavalry with C. Trebonius, the lieutenant, for the purpose of foraging, they flew upon the foragers suddenly from all quarters, so that they did not keep off [even] from the standards and the legions. Our men, making an attack on them vigorously, repulsed them; nor did they cease to pursue them until the horse, relying on relief, as they saw the legions behind them, drove the enemy precipitately before them, and, slaying a great number of them, did not give them the opportunity either of rallying, or halting, or leaping from their chariots. After this retreat the auxiliaries departed; nor after that time did the enemy ever engage with us in very large numbers.

Cæsar, discovering their design, leads his army into the territories of Cassivelaunus [8] to the river Thames, which river can be forded in one place only, and that with difficulty. When he had arrived there, he perceives that numerous forces of the enemy were marshaled on the other bank of the river; the bank also was defended by sharp stakes [9] fixt in front, and stakes of the

[8] Cassivelaunus was a chieftain of the Britons who had been entrusted with the supreme command against Cæsar. His own territory lay north of the Thames.

[9] Bede, the learned Benedictine, who lived in the eighth century, says that, in his time, remains of these stakes were still to be seen.

JULIUS CÆSAR

same kind fixt under the water were covered by the river. These things being discovered from [some] prisoners and deserters, Cæsar, sending forward the cavalry, ordered the legions to follow them immediately. But the soldiers advanced with such speed and such ardor, tho they stood above the water by their heads only, that the enemy could not sustain the attack of the legions and of the horse, and quitted the banks, and committed themselves to flight.

Cassivelaunus, as we have stated above, all hope [rising out] of battle being laid aside, the greater part of his forces being dismissed, and about 4,000 charioteers only being left, used to observe our marches and retire a little from the road, and conceal himself in intricate and woody places, and in those neighborhoods in which he had discovered we were about to march, he used to drive the cattle and the inhabitants from the fields into the woods; and, when our cavalry, for the sake of plundering and ravaging the more freely, scattered themselves among the fields, he used to send out charioteers from the woods by all the well-known roads and paths, and, to the great danger of our horse, engaged with them; and this source of fear hindered them from straggling very extensively. The result was that Cæsar did not allow excursions to be made to a great distance from the main body of the legions, and ordered that damage should be done to the enemy in ravaging their lands and kindling fires only so far as the legionary soldiers could, by their own exertion and marching, accomplish it.

In the mean time the Trinobantes,[10] almost the most powerful state of those parts, from which the young man Mandubratius, embracing the protection of Cæsar, had come to the continent of Gaul to [meet] him (whose father, Imanuentius, had possest the sovereignty in that state, and had been killed by Cassivelaunus; he himself had escaped death by flight) send ambassadors to Cæsar, and promise that they will surrender themselves to him and perform his command; they entreat him to protect Mandubratius from the violence of Cassivelaunus, and send to their state some one to preside over it, and possess the government. Cæsar demands forty hostages from them, and corn for his army, and sends Mandubratius to them. They speedily performed the things demanded, and sent hostages to the number appointed, and the corn.

The Trinobantes, being protected and secured from any violence of the soldiers, the Cenimagni, the Segontiăci, the Ancalites, the Bibrŏci, and the Cassi, sending embassies, surrender themselves to Cæsar.[11] From them he learns that the capital town of Cassivelaunus was not far from

---

[10] These people occupied what are now the counties of Essex and Middlesex.

[11] The translator notes that Tacitus has remarked that Britain was surveyed, rather than conquered, by Cæsar. He gives the honor of its real conquest to his own father-in-law, Agricola. While the Roman armies "owe much to the military virtues of Agricola as displayed in England, Cæsar," adds the translator, "did what no one had done before him; he levied tribute upon the Britons and effectually paved the way for all that Rome subsequently accomplished in this island."

that place, and was defended by woods and morasses, and a very large number of men and of cattle had been collected in it. (Now the Britons, when they have fortified the intricate woods, in which they are wont to assemble for the purpose of avoiding the incursion of an enemy with an entrenchment and a rampart, call them a town.) Thither he proceeds with his legions; he finds the place admirably fortified by nature and art; he, however, undertakes to attack it in two directions. The enemy, having remained only a short time, did not sustain the attack of our soldiers, and hurried away on the other side of the town. A great amount of cattle was found there, and many of the enemy were taken and slain in their flight. . . .

III

OVERCOMING THE NERVII[12]

Cæsar, having sent his cavalry on before, followed closely after them with all his forces; but the plan and order of the march were different from that which the Belgæ had reported to the Nervii.[13] For as he was approaching the enemy, Cæsar, according to his custom, led on [as the van] six legions unencumbered by baggage; behind them he had placed the baggage-trains of

[12] From Book II of the "Commentaries on the Gallic War."
[13] The Nervii were one of the Belgic tribes and are understood to have been the most warlike of them all.

the whole army; then the two legions which had been last raised closed the rear, and were a guard for the baggage-train. Our horse, with the slingers and archers, having passed the river, commenced action with the cavalry of the enemy. While they from time to time betook themselves into the woods to their companions, and again made an assault out of the wood upon our men, who did not dare to follow them in their retreat further than the limit to which the plain and open parts extended; in the mean time the six legions which had arrived first, having measured out the work, began to fortify the camp. When the first part of the baggage-train of our army was seen by those who lay hidden in the woods, which had been agreed on among them as the time for commencing action, as soon as they had arranged their line of battle and formed their ranks within the woods, and had encouraged one another, they rushed out suddenly with all their forces and made an attack upon our horse. The latter being easily routed and thrown into confusion, the Nervii ran down to the river with such incredible speed that they seemed to be in the woods, the river, and close upon us almost at the same time. And with the same speed they hastened up the hill to our camp and to those who were employed in the works.

Cæsar had everything to do at one time: the standard to be displayed, which was the sign when it was necessary to run to arms; the signal to be given by the trumpet; the soldiers to be called off from the works; those who had proceeded some distance for the purpose of seeking materials for the rampart, to be summoned; the

JULIUS CÆSAR

order of battle to be formed; the soldiers to be encouraged; the watchword to be given. A great part of these arrangements was prevented by the shortness of time and the sudden approach and charge of the enemy. Under these difficulties two things proved of advantage: [first] the skill and experience of the soldiers, because, having been trained by former engagements, they could suggest to themselves what ought to be done as conveniently as receive information from others; and [secondly] that Cæsar had forbidden his several lieutenants to depart from the works and their respective legions before the camp was fortified. These, on account of the near approach and the speed of the enemy, did not then wait for any command from Cæsar, but of themselves executed whatever appeared proper.

Cæsar, having given the necessary orders, hastened to and fro into whatever quarter fortune carried him, to animate the troops, and came to the tenth legion. Having encouraged the soldiers with no further speech than that "they should keep up the remembrance of their wonted valor, and not be confused in mind, but valiantly sustain the assault of the enemy"; as the latter were not farther from them than the distance to which a dart could be cast, he gave the signal for commencing battle. And having gone to another quarter for the purpose of encouraging [the soldiers], he finds them fighting. Such was the shortness of the time, and so determined was the mind of the enemy on fighting, that time was wanting not only for affixing the military insignia, but even for putting on the helmets and drawing off the covers from the shields. To whatever part any one by chance came from the works (in which he had been employed), and whatever standards he saw first, at these he stood, lest in seeking his own company he should lose the time for fighting.

The army having been marshaled, rather as the nature of the ground and the declivity of the hill and the exigency of the time than as the method and order of military matters required, while the legions in the different places were withstanding the enemy, some in one quarter, some in another, and the view was obstructed by the very thick hedges intervening, as we have before remarked, neither could proper reserves be posted, nor could the necessary measures be taken in each part, nor could all the commands be issued by one person. Therefore, in such an unfavorable state of affairs, various events of fortune followed. . . .

At the same time, our horsemen, and light-armed infantry, who had been with those who, as I have related, were routed by the first assault of the enemy, as they were betaking themselves into the camp, met the enemy face to face, and again sought flight into another quarter; and the camp-followers, who from the Decuman Gate, and from the highest ridge of the hill had seen our men pass the river as victors, when, after going out for the purposes of plundering, they looked back and saw the enemy parading in our camp, committed themselves precipitately to flight; at the same time there arose the cry and shout of those who came with the baggage-train; and they (affrighted) were carried some one

JULIUS CÆSAR

way, some another. By all these circumstances the cavalry of the Treviri were much alarmed (whose reputation for courage is extraordinary among the Gauls, and who had come to Cæsar, being sent by their state as auxiliaries), and, when they saw our camp filled with a large number of the enemy, the legions hard prest and almost held surrounded, the camp-retainers, horsemen, slingers, and Numidians fleeing on all sides divided and scattered, they, despairing of our affairs, hastened home, and related to their state that the Romans were routed and conquered, [and] that the enemy were in possession of their camp and baggage-train.

Cæsar proceeded, after encouraging the tenth legion, to the right wing, where he perceived that his men were hard prest, and that in consequence of the standards of the twelfth legion being collected together in one place, the crowded soldiers were a hindrance to themselves in the fight; that all the centurions of the fourth cohort were slain, and the standard-bearer killed, the standard itself lost, almost all the centurions of the other cohorts either wounded or slain, and among them the chief centurion of the legion, P. Sextius Baculus, a very valiant man, who was so exhausted by many and severe wounds that he was already unable to support himself; he likewise perceived that the rest were slackening their efforts, and that some, deserted by those in the rear, were retiring from the battle and avoiding the weapons; that the enemy [on the other hand], tho advancing from the lower ground, were not relaxing in front, and were [at the same time] pressing hard on both flanks; he perceived also that the affair was at a crisis, and that there was not any reserve which could be brought up; having therefore snatched a shield from one of the soldiers in the rear (for he himself had come without a shield), he advanced to the front of the line, and addressing the centurions by name, and encouraging the rest of the soldiers, he ordered them to carry forward the standards, and extend the companies, that they might the more easily use their swords. On his arrival, as hope was brought to the soldiers and their courage restored, while every one for his own part, in the sight of his general, desired to exert his utmost energy, the impetuosity of the enemy was a little checked.

Cæsar, when he perceived that the seventh legion, which stood close by him, was also hard prest by the enemy, directed the tribunes of the soldiers to effect a junction of the legions gradually, and make their charge upon the enemy with a double front, which having been done since they brought assistance the one to the other, nor feared lest their rear should be surrounded by the enemy, they began to stand their ground more boldly, and to fight more courageously. In the mean time, the soldiers of the two legions which had been in the rear of the army, as a guard for the baggage-train, upon the battle being reported to them, quickened their pace, and were seen by the enemy on the top of the hill; and Titus Labienus, having gained possession of the camp of the enemy, and observed from the higher ground what was going on in our camp, sent the tenth legion as a relief to our men, who, when they had learned from the flight of

JULIUS CÆSAR

the horse and the sutlers in what position the affair was, and in how great danger the camp and the legion and the commander were involved, left undone nothing [which tended] to despatch.

By their arrival, so great a change of matters was made that our men, even those who had fallen down exhausted with wounds, leaned on their shields, and renewed the fight; then the camp-retainers, tho unarmed, seeing the enemy completely dismayed, attacked [them tho] armed; the horsemen too, that they might by their valor blot out the disgrace of their flight, thrust themselves before the legionary soldiers in all parts of the battle. But the enemy, even in the last hope of safety, displayed such great courage that when the foremost of them had fallen, the next stood upon them prostrate, and fought from their bodies; when these were overthrown, and their corpses heaped up together, those who survived cast their weapons against our men [thence] as from a mound, and returned our darts which had fallen short between [the armies]; so that it ought not to be concluded that men of such great courage had injudiciously dared to pass a very broad river, ascend very high banks, and come up to a very disadvantageous place; since their greatness of spirit had rendered these actions easy, altho in themselves very difficult.

This battle being ended, and the nation and name of the Nervii being almost reduced to annihilation, their old men, who together with the boys and women we have stated to have been collected together in the fenny places and marshes, on this battle having been reported to them, since they were convinced that nothing was an obstacle to the conquerors, and nothing safe to the conquered, sent ambassadors to Cæsar by the consent of all who remained, and surrendered themselves to him; and in recounting the calamity of their state said that their senators were reduced from 600 to three; that from 60,000 men they [were reduced] to scarcely 500 who could bear arms, whom Cæsar, that he might appear to use compassion toward the wretched and the suppliant, most carefully spared, and ordered them to enjoy their own territories and towns, and commanded their neighbors that they should restrain themselves and their dependents from offering injury or outrage [to them]. . . .

IV

THE BATTLE OF PHARSALIA AND THE DEATH OF POMPEY[14]
(48 B.C.)

POMPEY, because he was encamped on a hill, drew up his army at the very foot of it, ever in expectation, as may be conjectured, that Cæsar would expose himself to this disadvantageous situation. Cæsar, seeing no likelihood of being able to bring Pompey to an action, judged it the

[14] From Book III of the "Commentaries on the Civil War." Pharsalia is a district of Thessaly in Greece. Cæsar's army numbered 22,000 legionaries and 1,000 cavalry; Pompey's, 45,000 legionaries and 7,000 cavalry.

JULIUS CÆSAR

most expedient method of conducting the war to decamp from that post, and to be always in motion; with this hope, that by shifting his camp and removing from place to place, he might be more conveniently supplied with corn, and also that by being in motion he might get some opportunity of forcing them to battle, and might by constant marches harass Pompey's army, which was not accustomed to fatigue.[15] These matters being settled, when the signal for marching was given, and the tents struck, it was observed that shortly before, contrary to his daily practise, Pompey's army had advanced farther than usual from his entrenchments, so that it appeared possible to come to an action on equal ground. Then Cæsar addrest himself to his soldiers, when they were at the gates of the camp, ready to march out. "We must defer," says he, "our march at present, and set our thoughts on battle, which has been our constant wish; let us then meet the foe with resolute souls. We shall not hereafter easily find such an opportunity." He immediately marched out at the head of his troops.

Pompey also, as was afterward known, at the unanimous solicitation of his friends, had determined to try the fate of a battle. For he had even declared in council a few days before that, before the battalions came to battle, Cæsar's army would be put to the rout. When most people exprest their surprize at it, "I know,"

---

[15] Pompey's army having been recruited from aristocratic families and their dependents, was not so much accustomed to the severities of war as were the soldiers of Cæsar, recruited largely from the populace.

says he, "that I promise a thing almost incredible; but hear the plan on which I proceed, that you may march to battle with more confidence and resolution. I have persuaded our cavalry, and they have engaged to execute it, as soon as the two armies have met, to attack Cæsar's right wing on the flank, and enclosing their army on the rear throw them into disorder, and put them to the rout, before we shall throw a weapon against the enemy. By this means we shall put an end to the war, without endangering the legions, and almost without a blow. Nor is this a difficult matter, as we far outnumber them in cavalry." At the same time, he gave them notice to be ready for battle on the day following, and since the opportunity which they had so often wished for was now arrived, not to disappoint the opinion generally entertained of their experience and valor. . . .

Cæsar, observing his former custom, had placed the tenth legion on the right, the ninth on the left, altho it was very much weakened by the battles at Dyrrachium.[16] He placed the eighth legion so close to the ninth as almost to make one of the two, and ordered them to support each other. He drew up on the field eighty cohorts, making a total of twenty-two thousand men. He left two cohorts to guard the camp. He gave the command of the left wing to Antonius, of the right to P. Sulla, and of the

---

[16] The modern Durazzo, a seaport on the Adriatic in Albania. It was founded by colonies from Corfu about 625 B.C. and became important afterward as a terminus of one of the great Roman roads. Pompey here defeated Cæsar a short time before he was himself defeated at Pharsalia.

JULIUS CÆSAR

center to Cn. Domitius; he himself took his post opposite Pompey. At the same time, fearing, from the disposition of the enemy which we have previously mentioned, lest his right wing might be surrounded by their numerous cavalry, he rapidly drafted a single cohort from each of the legions composing the third line, formed of them a fourth line, and opposed them to Pompey's cavalry, and, acquainting them with his wishes, admonished them that the success of that day depended on their courage. At the same time, he ordered the third line and the entire army not to charge without his command; that he would give the signal whenever he wished them to do so. . . .

But our men, when the signal was given, rushed forward with their javelins ready to be launched, but perceiving that Pompey's men did not run to meet their charge, having acquired experience by custom, and being practised in former battles, they of their own accord repressed their speed, and halted almost midway, that they might not come up with the enemy when their strength was exhausted, and after a short respite they again renewed their course, and threw their javelins, and instantly drew their swords, as Cæsar had ordered them. Nor did Pompey's men fail in this crisis, for they received our javelins, stood our charge, and maintained their ranks; and, having launched their javelins, had recourse to their swords. At the same time, Pompey's horse, according to their orders, rushed out at once from his left wing, and his whole host of archers poured after them. Our cavalry did not withstand their charge; but gave ground a little, upon which Pompey's horse prest them more vigorously, and began to file off in troops, and flank our army. When Cæsar perceived this, he gave the signal to his fourth line, which he had formed of the six cohorts. They instantly rushed forward and charged Pompey's horse with such fury that not a man of them stood; but all wheeling about, not only quitted their post, but galloped forward to seek a refuge in the highest mountains. By their retreat the archers and slingers, being left destitute and defenseless, were all cut to pieces. The cohorts, pursuing their success, wheeled about upon Pompey's left wing, while his infantry still continued to make battle, and attacked them in the rear.

At the same time, Cæsar ordered his third line to advance, which till then had not been engaged, but had kept their post. Thus, new and fresh troops having come to the assistance of the fatigued, and others having made an attack on their rear, Pompey's men were not able to maintain their ground, but all fled,[17] nor was Cæsar deceived in his opinion that the victory, as he had declared in his speech to his soldiers, must have its beginning from those six cohorts, which he had placed as a fourth line to oppose the horse. For by them the cavalry were routed; by them the archers and slingers were cut to pieces; by them the left wing of Pompey's army was surrounded, and obliged to be the

[17] Cæsar on this occasion is said to have advised his soldiers to aim at the faces of Pompey's cavalry, who, being composed principally of the young noblemen of Rome, dreaded a scar in the face more than death itself.

JULIUS CÆSAR

first to flee. But when Pompey saw his cavalry routed, and that part of his army on which he reposed his greatest hopes thrown into confusion, despairing of the rest, he quitted the field, and retreated straightway on horseback to his camp, and calling to the centurions, whom he had placed to guard the prætorian gate, with a loud voice, that the soldiers might hear: "Secure the camp," says he, "defend it with diligence, if any danger should threaten it; I will visit the other gates, and encourage the guards of the camp." Having thus said, he retired into his tent in utter despair, yet anxiously waiting the issue.

Cæsar having forced the Pompeians to flee into their entrenchment, and thinking that he ought not to allow them any respite to recover from their fright, exhorted his soldiers to take advantage of fortune's kindness, and to attack the camp. Tho they were fatigued by the intense heat, for the battle had continued till midday, yet, being prepared to undergo any labor, they cheerfully obeyed his command. The camp was bravely defended by the cohorts which had been left to guard it, but with much more spirit by the Thracians and foreign auxiliaries. For the soldiers who had fled for refuge to it from the field of battle, affrighted and exhausted by fatigue, having thrown away their arms and military standards, had their thoughts more engaged on their further escape than on the defense of the camp. Nor could the troops who were posted on the battlements long withstand the immense number of our darts, but fainting under their wounds quitted the place, and under the conduct of their centurions and tribunes fled, without stopping, to the high mountains which adjoined the camp.

In Pompey's camp you might see arbors in which tables were laid, a large quantity of plate set out, the floors of the tents covered with fresh sods, the tents of Lucius Lentulus and others shaded with ivy, and many other things which were proofs of excessive luxury, and a confidence of victory, so that it might readily be inferred that they had no apprehensions of the issue of the day, as they indulged themselves in unnecessary pleasures, and yet upbraided with luxury Cæsar's army, distrest and suffering troops, who had always been in want of common necessaries. Pompey, as soon as our men had forced the trenches, mounting his horse, and stripping off his general's habit, went hastily out of the back gate of the camp, and galloped with all speed to Larissa. Nor did he stop there, but with the same despatch, collecting a few of his flying troops, and halting neither day nor night, he arrived at the seaside, attended by only thirty horse, and went on board a victualing bark, often complaining, as we have been told, that he had been so deceived in his expectation that he was almost persuaded that he had been betrayed by those from whom he had expected victory, as they began the flight.

Cæsar, having possest himself of Pompey's camp, urged his soldiers not to be too intent on plunder, and lose the opportunity of completing their conquest. Having obtained their consent, he began to draw lines round the mountain. The Pompeians distrusting the position, as there was no water on the mountain, abandoned it, and all began to retreat toward Larissa, which Cæsar perceiving divided his troops, and ordering part of his legions to remain in Pompey's camp, sent back a part to his own camp, and, taking four legions with him, went by a shorter road to intercept the enemy; and having marched six miles, drew up his army. But the Pompeians, observing this, took a post on a mountain, whose foot was washed by a river. Cæsar having encouraged his troops, tho they were greatly exhausted by incessant labor the whole day, and night was now approaching, by throwing up works cut off the communication between the river and the mountain, that the enemy might not get water in the night. As soon as the work was finished, they sent ambassadors to treat about a capitulation. A few senators who had espoused that party made their escape by night.

At break of day, Cæsar ordered all those who had taken post on the mountain to come down from the higher grounds into the plain and pile their arms. When they did this without refusal, and, with outstretched arms, prostrating themselves on the ground, with tears, implored his mercy, he comforted them and bade them rise, and having spoken a few words of his own clemency to alleviate their fears, he pardoned them all, and gave orders to his soldiers that no injury should be done to them, and nothing taken from them. Having used this diligence, he ordered the legions in his camp to come and meet him, and those which were with him to take their turn of rest, and go back to the camp, and the same day went to Larissa.

In that battle, no more than two hundred privates were missing, but Cæsar lost about thirty centurions, valiant officers. Crastinus, also, of whom mention was made before, fighting most courageously, lost his life by the wound of a sword in the mouth, nor was that false which he declared when marching to battle; for Cæsar entertained the highest opinion of his behavior in that battle, and thought him highly deserving of his approbation. Of Pompey's army, there fell about fifteen thousand; but upward of twenty-four thousand were made prisoners: for even the cohorts which were stationed in the forts surrendered to Sulla. Several others took shelter in the neighboring states. One hundred and eighty stands of colors and nine eagles were brought to Cæsar. Lucius Domitius, fleeing from the camp to the mountains, his strength being exhausted by fatigue, was killed. . . .

Cæsar thought he ought to postpone all business and pursue Pompey, whithersoever he should retreat, that he might not be able to provide fresh forces, and renew the war; he therefore marched on every day, as far as his cavalry were able to advance, and ordered one legion to follow him by shorter journeys. A proclamation was issued by Pompey at Amphipolis [18] that all the young men of that province, Grecians and Roman citizens, should take the military oath; but whether he issued it with an intention of preventing suspicion, and to conceal as long as possible his design of fleeing farther, or to

[18] Amphipolis, a city of Macedonia, originally Thracian, but colonized from Athens. It was situated three miles inland from the Ægean Sea.

JULIUS CÆSAR

endeavor to keep possession of Macedonia by new levies, if nobody pursued him, it is impossible to judge. He lay at anchor one night, and calling together his friends in Amphipolis, and collecting a sum of money for his necessary expenses, upon advice of Cæsar's approach, set sail from that place, and arrived in a few days at Mitylene.[19] Here he was detained two days, and having added a few galleys to his fleet he went to Cilicia, and thence to Cyprus. There he is informed that, by the consent of all the inhabitants of Antioch[20] and Roman citizens who traded there, the castle had been seized to shut him out of the town; and that messengers had been dispatched to all those who were reported to have taken refuge in the neighboring states, that they should not come to Antioch; that if they did so, it would be attended with imminent danger to their lives. The same thing had happened to Lucius Lentulus, who had been Consul the year before, and to Publius Lentulus, a consular senator, and to several others at Rhodes,[21] who having followed Pompey in his

[19] Mitylene was the capital of the island of Lesbos, and an important maritime power in ancient times.

[20] Arrowsmith describes Antioch as, not only the capital of Syria, but at one time of Western Asia. It was for years the third city of the world in beauty, size, and population. It was here that the followers of Christ first received the name of Christians (in A.D. 39), having before been called Nazarenes and Galileans. In a neighboring grove stood a famous temple to Apollo and Diana.

[21] Rhodes is the largest island in the Ægean Sea after Crete and Eubœa. Its capital, having the same name and situated near the northern end of the island, was famous for a bronze statue of the sun called the Colossus, which was one of the "seven wonders of the world."

flight, and arrived at the island, were not admitted into the town or port; and having received a message to leave that neighborhood, set sail much against their will; for the rumor of Cæsar's approach had now reached those states.

Pompey, being informed of these proceedings, laid aside his design of going to Syria, and having taken the public money from the farmers of the revenue, and borrowed more from some private friends, and having put on board his ships a large quantity of brass for military purposes, and two thousand armed men, whom he partly selected from the slaves of the tax farmers, and partly collected from the merchants, and such persons as each of his friends thought fit on this occasion, he sailed for Pelusium.[22] It happened that King Ptolemy,[23] a minor, was there with a considerable army, engaged in war with his sister Cleopatra, whom a few months before, by the assistance of his relatives and friends, he had expelled from the kingdom; and her camp lay at a small distance from his. To him Pompey applied to be permitted to take refuge in Alexandria, and to be protected in his calamity by his powerful assistance, in consideration of the friendship and amity which had

---

[22] Pelusium was an ancient city of Egypt, situated in the delta of the Nile, strongly fortified and regarded as the gate to Egypt, on its eastern frontier. It lay in the midst of marshes formed by the overflow of the river, and continued its importance, in a military sense, until the waters of the river found their way into the Damietta branch.

[23] Ptolemy XII, who came to the throne of Egypt cojointly with his sister Cleopatra in 51 B.C. He expelled Cleopatra in 49, and in 48 Cæsar reinstated her. In the war which ensued, he was defeated and drowned in the Nile.

JULIUS CÆSAR

subsisted between his father and him. But Pompey's deputies, having executed their commission, began to converse with less restraint with the king's troops, and to advise them to act with friendship to Pompey, and not to think meanly of his bad fortune. In Ptolemy's army were several of Pompey's soldiers, of whom Gabinius[24] had received the command in Syria, and had brought them over to Alexandria, and at the conclusion of the war had left with Ptolemy the father of the young king.

The king's friends, who were regents of the kingdom during the minority, being informed of these things, either induced by fear, as they afterward declared, lest Pompey should corrupt the king's army, and seize on Alexandria[25] and Egypt, or despising his bad fortune, as in adversity friends commonly change to enemies, in public gave a favorable answer to his deputies, and desired him to come to the king; but secretly laid a plot against him, and dispatched Achillas, captain of the king's guards, a man of singular boldness, and Lucius Septimius, a military tribune, to assassinate him. Being kindly addrest by them, and deluded by an acquaintance with

[24] Gabinius was a Roman tribune who had proposed the statute bearing his name which gave to Pompey command of the Mediterranean coast for the suppression of pirates.

[25] Alexandria was founded in 331 B.C. by Alexander the Great. Its principal street, 2,000 feet wide, was adorned with "some of the most costly edifices and structures of marble which perhaps the world ever saw." Many of these marbles were subsequently taken to Rome and Constantinople. Alexandria for a long period was the center of commerce for all merchandise passing between Europe and the East. As a city of learning, it possest a famous library, which at one period comprized 700,000 volumes.

THE BEST OF THE WORLD'S CLASSICS

Septimius, because in the war with the pirates the latter had commanded a company under him, he embarked in a small boat, with a few attendants, and was there murdered by Achillas and Septimius. In like manner, Lucius Lentulus was seized by the king's order, and put to death in prison. . . .

SALLUST

Born in Italy about 86 B.C.; died about 34; elected tribune in 52; expelled from the Senate by the censors in 50, probably for being an active partizan of Cæsar; accompanied Cæsar on his African campaign in 46; became governor of Numidia, where he is said to have amassed a fortune unjustly; author of histories of the Catiline conspiracy and the war with Jugurtha.[1]

I

THE GENESIS OF CATILINE[2]

OF the city of Rome, as I understand, the founders and earliest inhabitants were the Trojans, who, under the conduct of Æneas, were wandering about as exiles from their country, without any settled abode; and with these were joined the Aborigines, a savage race of men, without laws or government, free, and owning

[1] Quintilian thought Sallust had rivaled Thucydides, but it has generally been held that he rather imitated him. The resemblance lies in the main in the language he employs. Crutwell remarks "that the deep insight of the Athenian into the connection of events is far removed from the popular rhetoric in which the Roman deplores the decline of virtue."

[2] From "The Conspiracy of Catiline." Translated by J. S. Watson. Catiline came of an old but impoverished patrician family. In the first Civil War, he had joined Sulla, and in the time of the proscription is said to have killed with his own hand his brother-in-law. In 67 B.C. he was governor of Africa; in 64 he joined P. Antronius in an attempt to murder the consuls-elect; in 64 he was himself defeated for the consulship.

no control. How easily these two tribes, tho of different origin, dissimilar language, and opposite habits of life, formed a union when they met within the same walls is almost incredible. But when their state, from an accession of population and territory and an improved condition of morals, showed itself tolerably flourishing and powerful, envy, as is generally the case in human affairs, was the consequence of its prosperity. The neighboring kings and people, accordingly, began to assail them in war, while a few only of their friends came to their support; for the rest, struck with alarm, shrunk from sharing their dangers. But the Romans, active at home and in the field, prepared with alacrity for their defense. They encouraged one another, and hurried to meet the enemy. They protected, with their arms, their liberty, their country, and their homes. And when they had at length repelled danger by valor, they lent assistance to their allies and supporters, and procured friendships rather by bestowing favors than by receiving them.

They had a government regulated by laws. The denomination of their government was monarchy. Chosen men, whose bodies might be enfeebled by years, but whose minds were vigorous in understanding, formed the council of the state; and these, whether from their age, or from the similarity of their duty, were called Fathers. But afterward, when the monarchical power, which had been originally established for the protection of liberty and for the promotion of the public interest, had degenerated into tyranny and oppression, they changed their plan, and appointed two magistrates, with power only annual; for they conceived that, by this method, the human mind would be least likely to grow overbearing through want of control.

At this period every citizen began to seek distinction, and to display his talents with greater freedom; for, with princes, the meritorious are greater objects of suspicion than the undeserving, and to them the worth of others is a source of alarm. But when liberty was secured, it is almost incredible how much the state strengthened itself in a short space of time, so strong a passion for distinction had pervaded it. Now, for the first time, the youth, as soon as they were able to bear the toils of war, acquired military skill by actual service in the camp, and took pleasure rather in splendid arms and military steeds than in the society of mistresses and convivial indulgence. To such men no toil was unusual, no place was difficult or inaccessible, no armed enemy was formidable; their valor had overcome everything. But among themselves the grand rivalry was for glory; each sought to be first to wound an enemy, to scale a wall, and to be noticed while performing such an exploit. Distinction such as this they regarded as wealth, honor, and true nobility. They were covetous of praise, but liberal of money; they desired competent riches, but boundless glory. I could mention, but that the account would draw me too far from my subject, places in which the Roman people, with a small body of men, routed vast armies of the enemy; and cities which, tho fortified by nature, they carried by assault. . . .

By these two virtues, intrepidity in war and equity in peace, they maintained themselves and their state; of their exercise of which virtues, I consider these as the greatest proofs: that, in war, punishment was oftener inflicted on those who attacked an enemy contrary to orders, and who, when commanded to retreat, retired too slowly from the contest, than on those who had dared to desert their standards, or, when prest by the enemy, to abandon their posts; and that, in peace, they governed more by conferring benefits than by exciting terror, and, when they received an injury, chose rather to pardon than to revenge it.

But when, by perseverance and integrity, the republic had increased its power; when mighty princes had been vanquished in war; when barbarous tribes and populous states had been reduced to subjection; when Carthage, the rival of Rome's dominion, had been utterly destroyed, and sea and land lay everywhere open to her sway, Fortune then began to exercise her tyranny, and to introduce universal innovation. To those who had easily endured toils, dangers, and doubtful and difficult circumstances, ease and wealth, the objects of desire to others, became a burden and a trouble. At first the love of money, and then that of power, began to prevail, and these became, as it were, the sources of every evil. For avarice subverted honesty, integrity, and other honorable principles, and in their stead, inculcated pride, inhumanity, contempt of religion, and general venality. Ambition prompted many to become deceitful; to keep one thing concealed in the breast, and another ready on the tongue; to estimate friendships and enmities, not by their worth, but according to interest; and to carry rather a specious countenance than an honest heart. These vices at first advanced but slowly, and were sometimes restrained by correction; but afterward, when their infection had spread like a pestilence, the state was entirely changed, and the government, from being the most equitable and praiseworthy, became rapacious and insupportable.

At first, however, it was ambition, rather than avarice, that influenced the minds of men—a vice which approaches nearer to virtue than the other. For of glory, honor, and power, the worthy is as desirous as the worthless; but the one pursues them by just methods; the other, being destitute of honorable qualities, works with fraud and deceit. But avarice has merely money for its object, which no wise man has ever immoderately desired. It is a vice which, as if imbued with deadly poison, enervates whatever is manly in body or mind. It is always unbounded and insatiable, and is abated neither by abundance nor by want.

But after Lucius Sulla, having recovered the government by force of arms, proceeded, after a fair commencement, to a pernicious termination, all became robbers and plunderers; some set their affections on houses, others on lands; his victorious troops knew neither restraint nor moderation, but inflicted on the citizens disgraceful and inhuman outrages. Their rapacity was increased by the circumstance that Sulla, in order to secure the attachment of the forces which he had commanded in Asia, had treated them, contrary to the practise of our ancestors, with extraordinary indulgence and exemption from discipline; and pleasant and luxurious quarters had easily, during seasons of idleness, enervated the minds of the soldiery. Then the armies of the Roman people first became habituated to licentiousness and intemperance, and began to admire statues, pictures, and sculptured vases; to seize such objects alike in public edifices and private dwellings; to spoil temples; and to cast off respect for everything, sacred and profane. Such troops, accordingly, when once they obtained the mastery, left nothing to the vanquished. Success unsettles the principles even of the wise, and scarcely would those of debauched habits use victory with moderation. . . .

In so populous and so corrupt a city, Catiline, as it was very easy to do, kept about him, like a body-guard, crowds of the unprincipled and desperate. For all those shameless, libertine, and profligate characters who had dissipated their patrimonies by gaming, luxury, and sensuality; all who had contracted heavy debts, to purchase immunity for their crimes or offenses; all assassins or sacrilegious persons from every quarter, convicted or dreading conviction for their evil deeds; all, besides, whom their tongue or their hand maintained by perjury or civil bloodshed; all, in fine, whom wickedness, poverty, or a guilty conscience disquieted, were the associates and intimate friends of Catiline. And if any one, as yet of unblemished character, fell into his society, he was presently rendered, by daily intercourse and temptation, similar and

SALLUST

equal to the rest. But it was the young whose acquaintance he chiefly courted, as their minds, ductile and unsettled from their age, were easily ensnared by his stratagems. For as the passions of each, according to his years, appeared excited, he furnished mistresses to some, bought horses and dogs for others, and spared, in a word, neither his purse nor his character, if he could but make them his devoted and trustworthy supporters. There were some, I know, who thought that the youth who frequented the house of Catiline were guilty of crimes against nature; but this report arose rather from other causes than from any evidence of the fact. . . .

Depending on such accomplices and adherents, and knowing that the load of debt was everywhere great, and that the veterans of Sulla,[3] having spent their money too liberally, and remembering their spoils and former victory, were longing for a civil war, Catiline formed the design of overthrowing the government. There was no army in Italy; Pompey was fighting in a distant part of the world;[4] he himself had great hopes of obtaining the consulship; the Senate was wholly off its guard; everything was quiet and tranquil, and all these circumstances were exceedingly favorable for Catiline. . . .

---

[3] These were men to whom Sulla had given land as rewards for services, but who from extravagance had fallen into debt. Cicero said nothing could help them but the resurrection of Sulla from the dead.

[4] Pompey was then conducting his campaign against Mithridates.

II

THE FATE OF THE CONSPIRATORS[5]

When the Senate, as I have stated, had gone over to the opinion of Cato, the Consul, thinking it best not to wait till night, which was coming on, lest any new attempts should be made during the interval, ordered the triumvirs to make such preparations as the execution of the conspirators required. He himself, having posted the necessary guards, conducted Lentulus[6] to the prison; and the same office was performed for the rest by the prætors.

There is a place in the prison, which is called the Tullian dungeon,[7] and which, after a slight ascent to the left, is sunk about twelve feet under ground. Walls secure it on every side, and over it is a vaulted roof connected with stone arches; but its appearance is disgusting and horrible, by reason of the filth, darkness, and stench. When Lentulus had been let down into this place, certain men, to whom orders had

---

[5] From "The Conspiracy of Catiline." Translated by J. S. Watson.

[6] Lentulus, who came of the ancient and noble Cornelian family, was one of the chiefs of the Catiline conspiracy. In 71 B.C. he was Consul, but in the next year was ejected from the Senate for "infamous life and manners."

[7] The Tullian dungeon at Rome was built by King Ancus Martius and enlarged by Servius Tullius, from whom it derived its name. It still exists as a subterranean chapel beneath the small church of San Pietro in Carcere. The church tradition is that St. Peter was imprisoned in this dungeon.

been given, strangled him with a cord. Thus this patrician who was of the illustrious family of the Cornelii, and who had filled the office of Consul at Rome, met with an end suited to his character and conduct. On Cethegus, Statilius, Gabinius, and Cœparius, punishment was inflicted in a similar manner.

During these proceedings at Rome, Catiline, out of the entire force which he himself had brought with him, and that which Manlius had previously collected, formed two legions, filling up the cohorts as far as his numbers would allow; and afterward, as any volunteers, or recruits from his confederates, arrived in his camp, he distributed them equally throughout the cohorts, and thus filled up his legions, in a short time, with their regular number of men, tho at first he had not had more than two thousand. But, of his whole army, only about a fourth part had the proper weapons of soldiers; the rest, as chance had equipped them, carried darts, spears, or sharpened stakes.

As Antonius[8] approached with his army, Cati-

---

[8] Not the triumvir, but his uncle, Caius Antonius, a man who after the conspiracy made a scandalous record, and in consequence was surnamed "Hybrida." He was Consul with Cicero, and is believed to have been one of the original Catiline conspirators, but Cicero gained him over to his own side by promising him the rich province of Macedonia. As Consul, Antonius was under the necessity of leading the army against Catiline; but, owing to unwillingness to fight against his former friend (Sallust says owing to lameness) he gave the immediate command on the day of battle to his legate, Petreius. The father of this Antonius and the grandfather of Mark Antony, the triumvir, was Mark Antony, the orator, frequently referred to by Cicero as one of the greatest of Roman orators.

line directed his march over the hills, encamping, at one time, in the direction of Rome, at another in that of Gaul. He gave the enemy no opportunity of fighting, yet hoped himself shortly to find one, if his accomplices at Rome should succeed in their objects. Slaves, meanwhile, of whom vast numbers had at first flocked to him, he continued to reject, not only as depending on the strength of the conspiracy, but as thinking it impolitic to appear to share the cause of citizens with runagates.

When it was reported in his camp, however, that the conspiracy had been discovered at Rome, and that Lentulus, Cethegus, and the rest whom I have named had been put to death, most of those whom the hope of plunder or the love of change had led to join in the war fell away. The remainder Catiline conducted, over rugged mountains and by forced marches, into the neighborhood of Pistoria, with a view to escape covertly, by crossroads, into Gaul.

But Quintus Metellus Celer, who, with a force of three legions, had, at that time, his station at Picenum, suspected that Catiline, from the difficulties of his position, would adopt precisely the course which we have just described. When, therefore, he had learned Catiline's route from some deserters, he immediately broke up his camp, and took his post at the very foot of the hills, at the point where Catiline's descent would be, in his hurried march into Gaul.[9] Nor was Antonius far distant, as he was pursuing, tho

[9] That is, northern Italy, which in ancient times had been occupied by Gallic people. Pistoria was an Etruscan town lying at the foot of the Apennines.

with a large army, yet through plainer ground, and with fewer hindrances, the enemy in retreat,

Catiline, when he saw that he was surrounded by mountains and by hostile forces, that his schemes in the city had been unsuccessful, and that there was no hope either of escape or of succor, thinking it best, in such circumstances, to try the fortune of a battle, resolved upon engaging, as speedily as possible, with Antonius. . . .

When he had spoken, he ordered, after a short delay, the signal for battle to be sounded, and led down his troops, in regular order, to the level ground. Having then sent away the horses of all the cavalry, in order to increase the men's courage by making their danger equal, he himself, on foot, drew up his troops suitably to their numbers and the nature of the ground. As a plain stretched between the mountains on the left, with a rugged rock on the right, he placed eight cohorts in front, and stationed the rest of his force, in close order, in the rear. From among these he removed all the ablest centurions, the veterans, and the stoutest of the common soldiers that were regularly armed into the foremost ranks. He ordered Caius Manlius to take the command on the right, and a certain officer of Fæsulæ on the left; while he himself, with his freedmen and the colonists, took his station by the eagle, which Caius Marius was said to have had in his army in the Cimbrian war.

On the other side, Caius Antonius, who, being lame, was unable to be present in the engagement, gave the command of the army to Marcus

Petreius, his lieutenant-general. Petreius ranged the cohorts of veterans, which he had raised to meet the present insurrection, in front, and behind them the rest of his force in lines. Then, riding round among his troops, and addressing his men by name, he encouraged them, and bade them remember that they were to fight against unarmed marauders, in defense of their country, their children, their temples, and their homes. Being a military man, and having served with great reputation for more than thirty years, as tribune, prefect, lieutenant, or prætor, he knew most of the soldiers and their honorable actions, and, by calling these to their remembrance, roused the spirits of the men.

When he had made a complete survey, he gave the signal with the trumpet, and ordered the cohorts to advance slowly. The army of the enemy followed his example; and when they had approached so near that the action could be commenced by the light-armed troops, both sides, with a loud shout, rushed together in a furious charge. They threw aside their missiles, and fought only with their swords. The veterans, calling to mind their deeds of old, engaged fiercely in the closest combat. The enemy made an obstinate resistance; and both sides contended with the utmost fury. Catiline, during this time, was exerting himself with his light troops in the front, sustaining such as were prest, substituting fresh men for the wounded, attending to every exigency, charging in person, wounding many an enemy, and performing at once the duties of a valiant soldier and a skilful general.

SALLUST

When Petreius, contrary to his expectation, found Catiline attacking him with such impetuosity, he led his prætorian cohort against the center of the enemy, among whom, being thus thrown into confusion, and offering but partial resistance, he made great slaughter, and ordered, at the same time, an assault on both flanks. Manlius and the Fæsulan, sword in hand, were among the first that fell; and Catiline, when he saw his army routed, and himself left with but few supporters, remembering his birth and former dignity, rushed into the thickest of the enemy, where he was slain, fighting to the last.

When the battle was over, it was plainly seen what boldness and what energy of spirit had prevailed throughout the army of Catiline; for, almost everywhere, every soldier, after yielding up his breath, covered with his corpse the spot which he had occupied when alive. A few, indeed, whom the prætorian cohort had dispersed, had fallen somewhat differently, but all with wounds in front. Catiline himself was found, far in advance of his men, among the dead bodies of the enemy; he still breathed, and exprest in his countenance the fierceness of spirit which he had shown during his life. Of his whole army, neither in the battle, nor in flight, was any free-born citizen made prisoner, for they had spared their own lives no more than those of the enemy.

Nor did the army of the Roman people obtain a joyful or bloodless victory; for all their bravest men were either killed in the battle or left the field severely wounded.

Of many who went from the camp to view

the ground or plunder the slain, some, in turning over the bodies of the enemy, discovered a friend, others an acquaintance, others a relative; some, too, recognized their enemies. Thus, gladness and sorrow, grief and joy, were variously felt throughout the whole army.

LIVY

Born in Padua in 59 B.C.; died there in 17 A.D.; one of the most famous of the Roman historians; his work, embracing the period from the founding of the city, comprized one hundred and forty-two books, of which only thirty-five have come down to us; he spent over forty years in writing the history; he wrote also philosophical dialogs and a work on rhetorical training.[1]

I

HORATIUS COCLES AT THE BRIDGE[2]
(About 510 B.C.)

THE Sublician bridge[3] well-nigh afforded a passage to the enemy, had it not been for one man, Horatius Cocles, given by fortune on that day as a defense of Rome. He happened to be posted on guard at the bridge and when he saw the Janiculum taken by a sudden assault, and that the enemy were pouring down thence in full speed, and that his own party in terror and confusion were abandoning their arms and ranks

---

[1] "The most eloquent of all historians," says Cruttwell. Livy understood the spirit of ancient times, making it real to modern minds because he possest "antiquity of soul." In his own day Livy's popularity was almost limitless. Pliny the Younger recalled that a man once traveled to Rome from Cadiz with the express purpose of seeing Livy. Having seen him he returned home at once, caring for nothing else in Rome.

[2] From Book II of the "History of Rome." Translated by D. Spillan and Cyrus Edmonds. "Cocles" was a nick-

THE BEST OF THE WORLD'S CLASSICS

—laying hold of them one by one, standing in their way, and appealing to the faith of gods and men, he declared "that their flight would avail them nothing if they deserted their post; if they passed the bridge and left it behind them, there would soon be more of the enemy in the Palatium and Capitol than in the Janiculum; for that reason he advised and charged them to demolish the bridge, by their sword, by fire, or by any means whatever; that he would stand the shock of the enemy as far as could be done by one man."

He then advanced to the first entrance of the bridge, and being easily distinguished among those who showed their backs in retreating from the fight, facing about to engage the foe hand to hand, by his surprising bravery he terrified the enemy. Two indeed a sense of shame kept with him—Spurius Lartius and Titus Herminius—men eminent for their birth, and renowned for their gallant exploits.

---

name meaning the "one-eyed." With this story every schoolboy has been made familiar through Macaulay's "Lay," beginning:

"Lars Porsena of Clusium
By the Nine Gods he swore
That the great house of Tarquin
Should suffer wrong no more."

[3] Authorities differ as to the site of this bridge. "Larousse" has a map which identifies it as the site now occupied by the Æmilian bridge, at the base of the Palatine, near the mouth of the Cloaca Maxima; but the "Encyclopædia Britannica," in a map of ancient Rome, places it farther down the Tiber near the center of the base of the Aventine. Murray's "Handbook of Rome" agrees with the "Britannica." This bridge was the first one built at Rome, and is ascribed to King Ancus Martius.

With them he for a short time stood the first storm of the danger, and the severest brunt of the battle. But as they who demolished the bridge called upon them to retire, he obliged them also to withdraw to a place of safety on a small portion of the bridge still left. Then casting his stern eyes round all the officers of the Etrurians in a threatening manner, he sometimes challenged them singly, sometimes reproached them all: "the slaves of haughty tyrants, who, regardless of their own freedom, came to oppress the liberty of others." They hesitated for a considerable time, looking round one at the other, to commence the fight; shame then put the army in motion, and a shout being raised, they hurled their weapons from all sides on their single adversary; and when they all stuck in the shield held before him, and he with no less obstinacy kept possession of the bridge with firm step, they now endeavored to thrust him down from it by one push, when at once the crash of the falling bridge, at the same time a shout of the Romans raised for joy at having completed their purpose, checked their ardor with sudden panic. Then Cocles says, "Holy father Tiberinus, I pray that thou wouldst receive these arms and this thy soldier in thy propitious stream." Armed as he was, he leapt into the Tiber, and, amid showers of darts hurled on him, swam across safe to his party, having dared an act which is likely to obtain more fame than belief with posterity. The state was grateful toward such valor; a statue was erected to him in the Comitium, and as much land was given to him as he plowed around in one day.

The zeal of private individuals also was conspicuous among the public honors. For amid the great scarcity, each person contributed something to him according to his supply at home, depriving himself of his own support.

II

HANNIBAL'S CROSSING OF THE ALPS[4]
(218 B.C.)

FROM the Druentia, by a road that lay principally through plains, Hannibal arrived at the Alps without molestation from the Gauls who inhabit those regions. Then, tho the scene had been previously anticipated from report (by which uncertainties are wont to be exaggerated), yet the height of the mountains when viewed so near, and the snows almost mingling with the sky, the shapeless huts situated on the cliffs, the cattle and beasts of burden withered by the cold, the men unshorn and wildly drest, all things, animate and inanimate, stiffened with frost, and other objects more terrible to be seen than described, renewed their alarm.

To them, marching up the first acclivities, the mountaineers appeared occupying the heights

[4] From Book XXI of the "History of Rome." Translated by D. Spillan and Cyrus Edmonds. The identity of the pass through which Hannibal crossed has been the subject of much controversy. A writer in Smith's "Dictionary" says the account in Polybius "will be found, on the whole, to agree best with the supposition that Hannibal crossed by the Little St. Bernard." At the same time, "there are some difficulties" attending this inference.

overhead, who, if they had occupied the more concealed valleys, might, by rushing out suddenly to the attack, have occasioned great flight and havoc. Hannibal orders them to halt, and having sent forward Gauls to view the ground, when he found there was no passage that way, he pitches his camp in the widest valley he could find, among places all rugged and precipitous. Then, having learned from the same Gauls, when they had mixed in conversation with the mountaineers, from whom they differed little in language and manners, that the pass was only beset during the day, and that at night each withdrew to his own dwelling, he advanced at the dawn to the heights, as if designing openly and by day to force his way through the defile. The day then being passed in feigning a different attempt from that which was in preparation, when they had fortified the camp in the same place where they had halted, as soon as he perceived that the mountaineers had descended from the heights, and that the guards were withdrawn, having lighted for show a greater number of fires than was proportioned to the number that remained, and having left the baggage in the camp, with the cavalry and the principal part of the infantry, he himself with a party of light-armed soldiers, consisting of all the most courageous of his troops, rapidly cleared the defile, and took posts on those very heights which the enemy had occupied.

At dawn of light the next day the camp broke up, and the rest of the army began to move forward. The mountaineers, on a signal being given, were now assembling from their forts to their usual station, when they suddenly behold part of the enemy overhanging them from above, in possession of their former position, and the others passing along the road. Both these objects, presented at the same time to the eye and the mind, made them stand motionless for a little while; but when they afterward saw the confusion in the pass, and that the marching body was thrown into disorder by the tumult which itself created, principally from the horses being terrified, thinking that whatever terror they added would suffice for the destruction of the enemy, they scramble along the dangerous rocks, as being accustomed alike to pathless and circuitous ways. Then indeed the Carthaginians were opposed at once by the enemy and by the difficulties of the ground; and each striving to escape first from the danger, there was more fighting among themselves than with their opponents. The horses, in particular, created danger in the lines, which being terrified by the discordant clamors that the groves and reechoing valleys augmented, fell into confusion; and if by chance struck or wounded, they were so dismayed that they occasioned a great loss both of men and baggage of every description; and as the pass on both sides was broken and precipitous, this tumult threw many down to an immense depth, some even of the armed men; but the beasts of burden, with their loads, were rolled down like the fall of some vast fabric.

Tho these disasters were shocking to view, Hannibal, however, held his place for a little, and kept his men together, lest he might augment the tumult and disorder: but afterward, when he saw the line broken, and that there was danger that he should bring over his army preserved to no purpose if deprived of their baggage, he hastened down from the higher ground; and tho he had routed the enemy by the first onset alone, he at the same time increased the disorder in his own army; but that tumult was composed in a moment, after the roads were cleared by the flight of the mountaineers, and presently the whole army was conducted through, not only without being disturbed, but almost in silence. He then took a fortified place, which was the capital of that district, and the little villages that lay around it, and fed his army for three days with the corn and cattle he had taken; and during these three days, as the soldiers were neither obstructed by the mountaineers, who had been daunted by the first engagement, nor yet much by the ground, he made considerable way.

He then came to another state, abounding, for a mountainous country, with inhabitants, where he was nearly overcome, not by open war, but by his own arts of treachery and ambuscade. Some old men, governors of forts, came as deputies to the Carthaginian, professing, "that having been warned by the useful example of the calamities of others, they wished rather to experience the friendship than the hostilities of the Carthaginians; they would, therefore, obediently execute his commands, and begged that he would accept of a supply of provisions, guides of his march, and hostages for the sincerity of their promises." Hannibal, when he had answered them in a friendly manner, thinking that they should neither be rashly trusted nor yet rejected, lest if repulsed they might openly become enemies, having received the hostages whom they proffered, and made use of the provisions which they of their own accord brought down to the road, followed their guides, by no means as among a people with whom he was at peace, but with his line of march in close order. The elephants and cavalry formed the van of the marching body; he himself, examining everything around, and intent on every circumstance, followed with the choicest of his infantry. When they came into a narrower pass, lying on one side beneath an overhanging eminence, the barbarians, rising at once on all sides from their ambush, assail them in front and rear, both at close quarters and from a distance, and roll down huge stones on the army. The most numerous body of men prest on the rear; against whom the infantry facing about and directing their attack made it very obvious that, had not the rear of the army been well supported, a great loss must have been sustained in that pass. Even as it was, they came to the extremity of danger, and almost to destruction; for while Hannibal hesitated to lead down his division into the defile, because, tho he himself was a protection to the cavalry, he had not in the same way left any aid to the infantry in the rear; the mountaineers, charging obliquely, and on having broken through the middle of the army, took possession of the road; and one night was spent by Hannibal without his cavalry and baggage. . . .

On the standards being moved forward at daybreak, when the army proceeded slowly over all places entirely blocked up with snow, and languor and despair strongly appeared in the countenances of all, Hannibal, having advanced before the standards, and ordered the soldiers to halt on a certain eminence, whence there was a prospect far and wide, pointed out to them Italy and the plains of the Po, extending themselves beneath the Alpine mountains; and said "that they were now surmounting not only the ramparts of Italy, but also of the city of Rome; that the rest of the journey would be smooth and down-hill; that after one, or, at most, a second battle, they would have the citadel and capital of Italy in their power and possession." The army then began to advance, the enemy now making no attempts beyond petty thefts, as opportunity offered. But the journey proved much more difficult than it had been in the ascent, as the declivity of the Alps, being generally shorter on the side of Italy, is consequently steeper; for nearly all the road was precipitous, narrow, and slippery, so that neither those who made the least stumble could prevent themselves from falling, nor, when fallen, remain in the same place, but rolled, both men and beasts of burden, one upon another.

They then came to a rock much more narrow, and formed of such perpendicular ledges that a light-armed soldier, carefully making the attempt, and clinging with his hands to the bushes and roots around, could with difficulty lower himself down. The ground, even before very steep by nature, had been broken by a recent falling away of the earth into a precipice of nearly a thousand feet in depth. Here when the cavalry halted, as if at the end of their journey, it was announced to Hannibal, wondering what obstructed the march, that the rock was impassable.

Having then gone himself to view the place, it seemed clear to him that he must lead his army, by however great a circuit, through the pathless and untrodden regions around it. But this route also proved impracticable; for while the new snow of a moderate depth remained on the old, which had not been removed, their footsteps were planted with ease as they walked upon the new snow, which was soft and not too deep; but when it was dissolved by the trampling of so many men and beasts of burden, they then walked on the bare ice below, and through the dirty fluid formed by the melting snow. Here there was a wretched struggle, both on account of the slippery ice not affording any hold to the step, and giving way beneath the foot more readily by reason of the slope; and whether they assisted themselves in rising by their hands or their knees, their supports themselves giving way, they would tumble again; nor were there any stumps or roots near by pressing against which one might with hand or foot support oneself; so that they only floundered on the smooth ice and amidst the melted snow. The beasts of burden sometimes also cut into this lower ice by merely treading upon it, at others they broke it completely through, by the violence with which they struck in their hoofs in their struggling, so that most of them, as if taken in a trap, stuck in the hardened and deeply frozen ice.

At length, after the men and beasts of burden had been fatigued to no purpose, the camp was pitched on the summit, the ground being cleared for that purpose with great difficulty, so much snow was there to be dug out and carried away. The soldiers being then set to make a way down the cliff, by which alone a passage could be effected, and it being necessary that they should cut through the rocks, having felled and lopped a number of large trees which grew around, they make a huge pile of timber; and as soon as a strong wind fit for exciting the flames arose, they set fire to it, and, pouring vinegar on the heated stones, they render them soft and crumbling. They then open a way with iron instruments through the rock thus heated by the fire, and soften its declivities by gentle windings, so that not only the beasts of burden, but also the elephants, could be led down it. Four days were spent about this rock, the beasts nearly perishing through hunger; for the summits of the mountains are for the most part bare, and if there is any pasture the snows bury it. The lower parts contain valleys, and some sunny hills, and rivulets flowing beside woods, and scenes more worthy of the abode of man. There the beasts of burden were sent out to pasture, and rest given for three days to the men, fatigued with forming the passage; they then descended into the plains, the country and the dispositions of the inhabitants being now less rugged.

In this manner chiefly they came to Italy, in the fifth month (as some authors relate) after leaving New Carthage, having crossed the Alps in fifteen days. What number of forces Hannibal had when he had passed into Italy is by no means agreed upon by authors. Those who state them at the highest make mention of a hundred thousand foot and twenty thousand horse; those who state them at the lowest, of twenty thousand foot and six thousand horse. Lucius Cincius Alimentus, who relates that he was made prisoner by Hannibal, would influence me most as an authority did he not confound the number by adding the Gauls and Ligurians. Including these (who, it is more probable, flocked to him afterward, as some authors assert), he says that eighty thousand foot and ten thousand horse were brought into Italy; and that he had heard from Hannibal himself that, after crossing the Rhone, he had lost thirty-six thousand men, and an immense number of horses and other beasts of burden among the Taurini,[5] the next nation to the Gauls, as he descended into Italy.

[5] A tribe living in the upper valley of the Po, near Turin.

III

HANNIBAL AND SCIPIO AT ZAMA[6]
(202 B.C.)

HANNIBAL had by this time arrived at Adrumetum,[7] from which place, after employing a few days there in refreshing his soldiers, who had suffered from the motion by sea, he proceeded by forced marches to Zama, roused by the alarming statements of messengers, who brought word that all the country round Carthage was filled with armed troops. Zama is distant from Carthage a five days' journey. Some spies, whom he had sent out from this place, being intercepted by the Roman guard, and brought before Scipio, he directed that they should be handed over to the military tribunes, and, after having been desired fearlessly to survey everything, he conducted them through the camp wherever they chose; then, asking them whether they had examined everything to their satisfaction, he assigned them an escort, and sent them back to Hannibal. Hannibal received none of the circumstances which were reported to him with feelings of joy; for they brought word that, as it happened, Masinissa had joined the enemy that very day, with six thousand infantry and

[6] From Book XXX of the "History of Rome." Translated by D. Spillan and Cyrus Edmonds.

[7] Adrumetum lay in what is now Tunis and was originally a Phenician city. It was older than Carthage. For many centuries it was a chief seaport for northern Africa. It is now known as Susa.

four thousand horse; but he was principally dispirited by the confidence of his enemy, which, doubtless, was not conceived without some ground. Accordingly, tho he himself was the originator of the war, and by his coming had upset the truce which had been entered into, and cut off all hopes of a treaty, yet, concluding that more favorable terms might be obtained if he solicited peace while his strength was unimpaired than when vanquished, he sent a message to Scipio requesting permission to confer with him.

Their armed attendants having retired to an equal distance, they met, each attended by one interpreter, being the greatest generals not only of their own times, but of any to be found in the records of the times preceding them, and equal to any of the kings or generals of any nation whatever. When they came within sight of each other they remained silent for a short time, thunderstruck, as it were, with mutual admiration. At length Hannibal thus began:

"Since fate hath so ordained it, that I, who was the first to wage war upon the Romans, and who have so often had victory almost within my reach, should voluntarily come to sue for peace, I rejoice that it is you, above all others, from whom it is my lot to solicit it. To you, also, amidst the many distinguished events of your life, it will not be esteemed one of the least glorious that Hannibal, to whom the gods had so often granted victory over the Roman generals, should have yielded to you; and that you should have put an end to this war, which has been rendered remarkable by your calamities before it was by ours. In this, also, fortune would seem to have exhibited a disposition to sport with events, for it was when your father was Consul that I first took up arms; he was the first Roman general with whom I engaged in a pitched battle; and it is to his son that I now come unarmed to solicit peace. It were, indeed, most to have been desired that the gods should have put such dispositions into the minds of our fathers, that you should have been content with the empire of Italy, and we with that of Africa; nor, indeed, even to you, are Sicily and Sardinia of sufficient value to compensate you for the loss of so many fleets, so many armies, so many and such distinguished generals.

"But what is past may be more easily censured than retrieved. In our attempts to acquire the possessions of others, we have been compelled to fight for our own; and not only have you had a war in Italy, and we also in Africa, but you have beheld the standards and arms of your enemies almost in your gates and on your walls, and we now, from the walls of Carthage, distinctly hear the din of a Roman camp. What, therefore, we should most earnestly deprecate, and you should most devoutly wish for, is now the case: peace is proposed at a time when you have the advantage. We who negotiate it are the persons whom it most concerns to obtain it, and we are persons whose arrangements, be they what they will, our states will ratify. All we want is a disposition not averse from peaceful counsels. So far as relates to myself, time (for I am returning to that country an old man which

I left a boy),[8] and prosperity, and adversity, have so schooled me that I am more inclined to follow reason than fortune. But I fear your youth and uninterrupted good fortune, both of which are apt to inspire a degree of confidence ill comporting with pacific counsels. Rarely does that man consider the uncertainty of events whom fortune hath never deceived. What I was at Trasimenus and at Cannæ that you are this day. Invested with command when you had scarcely yet attained the military age, tho all your enterprises were of the boldest description, in no instance has fortune deserted you. Avenging the death of your father and uncle, you have derived from the calamity of your house the high honor of distinguished valor and filial duty. You have recovered Spain, which had been lost, after driving thence four Carthaginian armies. When elected Consul, tho all others wanted courage to defend Italy, you crossed over into Africa, where, having cut to pieces two armies, having at once captured and burned two camps in the same hour, having made prisoner Syphax, a most powerful king, and seized so many towns of his dominions and so many of ours, you have dragged me from Italy, the possession of which I had firmly held for now sixteen years. . . .

"Formerly, in this same country, Marcus Atilius would have formed one among the few instances of good fortune and valor, if, when vic-

[8] Hannibal, who when a boy of nine had left Carthage for Spain with his father, Hamilcar Barca, at that time took an oath upon an altar declaring eternal hostility to Rome. In the year of Zama he was forty-five years old.

torious, he had granted a peace to our fathers when they requested it; but by not setting any bounds to his success, and not checking good fortune, which was elating him, he fell with a degree of ignominy proportioned to his elevation. It is, indeed, the right of him who grants, and not of him who solicits it, to dictate the terms of peace; but perhaps we may not be unworthy to impose upon ourselves the fine. We do not refuse that all those possessions on account of which the war was begun should be yours—Sicily, Sardinia, Spain, with all the islands lying in any part of the sea, between Africa and Italy. Let us Carthaginians, confined within the shores of Africa, behold you, since such is the pleasure of the gods, extending your empire over foreign nations, both by sea and land. I can not deny that you have reason to suspect the Carthaginian faith, in consequence of their insincerity lately in soliciting a peace and while awaiting the decision. The sincerity with which a peace will be observed depends much, Scipio, on the person by whom it is sought. Your Senate, as I hear, refused to grant a peace, in some measure, because the deputies were deficient in respectability. It is I, Hannibal, who now solicit peace, who would neither ask for it unless I believed it expedient, nor will I fail to observe it for the same reason of expedience on account of which I have solicited it. And in the same manner as I, because the war was commenced by me, brought it to pass that no one regretted it till the gods began to regard me with displeasure, so will I also exert myself that no one may regret the peace procured by my means."

In answer to these things the Roman general spoke nearly to the following effect:

"I was aware that it was in consequence of the expectation of your arrival that the Carthaginians violated the existing faith of the truce and broke off all hope of a peace. Nor, indeed, do you conceal the fact; inasmuch as you artfully withdraw from the former conditions of peace every concession except what relates to those things which have for a long time been in our own power. But as it is your object that your countrymen should be sensible how great a burden they are relieved from by your means, so it is incumbent upon me to endeavor that they may not receive, as the reward of their perfidy, the concessions which they formerly stipulated, by expunging them now from the conditions of the peace. Tho you do not deserve to be allowed the same conditions as before, you now request even to be benefited by your treachery. Neither did our fathers first make war respecting Sicily, nor did we respecting Spain. In the former case, the danger which threatened our allies, the Mamertines, and in the present the destruction of Saguntum, girded us with just and pious arms. That you were the aggressors, both you yourselves confess and the gods are witnesses, who determined the issue of the former war, and who are now determining, and will determine, the issue of the present according to right and justice. As to myself, I am not forgetful of the instability of human affairs, but consider the influence of fortune, and am well aware that all our measures are liable to a thousand casualties. But as I should acknowledge that my conduct would savor of insolence and oppression if I rejected you on your coming in person to solicit peace, before I crossed over into Africa, you voluntarily retiring from Italy, and after you had embarked your troops, so now, when I have dragged you into Africa almost by manual force, notwithstanding your resistance and evasions, I am not bound to treat you with any respect. Wherefore, if in addition to those stipulations on which it was considered that a peace would at that time have been agreed upon, and what they are you are informed, a compensation is proposed for having seized our ships, together with their stores, during a truce, and for the violence offered to our ambassadors, I shall then have matter to lay before my council. But if these things also appear oppressive, prepare for war, since you could not brook the conditions of peace.''

Thus, without effecting an accommodation, when they had returned from the conference to their armies, they informed them that words had been bandied to no purpose, that the question must be decided by arms, and that they must accept that fortune which the gods assigned them.

When they had arrived at their camps, they both issued orders that their soldiers should get their arms in readiness and prepare their minds for the final contest; in which, if fortune should favor them, they would continue victorious, not for a single day, but forever. "Before tomorrow night," they said, "they would know whether Rome or Carthage should give laws to the world; and that neither Africa nor Italy, but the whole world, would be the prize of victory; that the dangers which threatened those who had the misfortune to be defeated were proportioned to the rewards of the victors.'' For the Romans had not any place of refuge in an unknown and foreign land, and immediate destruction seemed to await Carthage if the troops which formed her last reliance were defeated. To this important contest, the day following, two generals, by far the most renowned of any, and belonging to two of the most powerful nations in the world, advanced either to crown or overthrow, on that day, the many honors they had previously acquired. . . .

While the general was busily employed among the Carthaginians, and the captains of the respective nations among their countrymen, most of them employing interpreters among troops intermixed with those of different nations, the trumpets and cornets of the Romans sounded; and such a clamor arose that the elephants, especially those in the left wing, turned round upon their own party, the Moors and Numidians. Masinissa had no difficulty in increasing the alarm of the terrified enemy, and deprived them of the aid of their cavalry in that wing. A few, however, of the beasts which were driven against the enemy, and were not turned back through fear, made great havoc among the ranks of the velites, tho not without receiving many wounds themselves; for when the velites, retiring to the companies, had made way for the elephants, that they might not be trampled down, they discharged their darts at the beasts, exposed as they were to wounds on both sides, those in the van also keeping up a continual discharge of javelins; until, driven out of the Roman line by the weapons which fell upon them from all quarters, these elephants also put to flight even the cavalry of the Carthaginians posted in their right wing. Lælius, when he saw the enemy in disorder, struck additional terror into them in their confusion.

The Carthaginian line was deprived of the cavalry on both sides, when the infantry, who were now not a match for the Romans in confidence or strength, engaged. In addition to this there was one circumstance, trifling in itself, but at the same time producing important consequences in the action. On the part of the Romans the shout was uniform, and on that account louder and more terrific; while the voices of the enemy, consisting as they did of many nations of different languages, were dissonant. The Romans used the stationary kind of fight, pressing upon the enemy with their own weight and that of their arms; but on the other side there was more of skirmishing and rapid movement than force.

Accordingly, on the first charge, the Romans immediately drove back the line of their opponents; then pushing them with their elbows and the bosses of their shields, and pressing forward into the places from which they had pushed them, they advanced a considerable space, as tho there had been no one to resist them, those who formed the rear urging forward those in front when they perceived the line of the enemy giving way, which circumstance itself gave great additional force in repelling them. On the side of the enemy, the second line, consisting of the Africans and Carthaginians, were so far from supporting the first line when giving ground, that, on the contrary, they even retired, lest their enemy, by slaying those who made a firm resistance, should penetrate to themselves also. Accordingly, the auxiliaries suddenly turned their backs, and facing about upon their own party, fled some of them into the second line, while others slew those who did not receive them into their ranks, since before they did not support them, and now refused to receive them.

And now there were, in a manner, two contests going on together, the Carthaginians being compelled to fight at once with the enemy and with their own party. Not even then, however, did they receive into their line the terrified and exasperated troops; but, closing their ranks, drove them out of the scene of action to the wings and the surrounding plain, lest they should mingle these soldiers, terrified with defeat and wounds, with that part of their line which was firm and fresh. But such a heap of men and arms had filled the space in which the auxiliaries a little while ago had stood that it was almost more difficult to pass through it than through a close line of troops. The spearmen, therefore, who formed the front line, pursuing the enemy as each could find a way through the heap of arms and men, and streams of blood, threw into complete disorder the battalions and companies. The standards, also, of the principes had begun to waver when they saw the line before them driven from their ground. Scipio, perceiving this, promptly ordered the signal to be given for the spearmen to retreat, and, having taken his wounded into the rear, brought the principes and triarii to the wings, in order that the line of spearmen in the center might be more strong and secure. Thus a fresh and renewed battle commenced, inasmuch as they had penetrated to their real antagonists, men equal to them in the nature of their arms, in their experience in war, in the fame of their achievements, and the greatness of their hopes and fears. But the Romans were superior both in numbers and courage, for they had now routed both the cavalry and the elephants, and, having already defeated the front line, were fighting against the second. . . .

Hannibal, after performing this, as it were, his last work of valor, fled to Adrumetum, whence, having been summoned to Carthage, he returned thither in the six and thirtieth year after he had left it when a boy, and confest in the senate house that he was defeated, not only in the battle, but in the war, and that there was no hope of safety in anything but obtaining peace.

SENECA

Born in Spain about 4 B.C.; died near Rome in 65 A.D.; celebrated as a Stoic and writer; taken to Rome when a child; a senator in Caligula's reign; banished to Corsica by Claudius in 41; recalled in 49, and entrusted with the education of Nero; after Nero's accession in 54 virtually controlled the imperial government, exercising power in concert with the Prætorian prefect, Burrus; on the assassination of Burrus in 62 petitioned for leave to retire from court, and virtually did withdraw; on being charged with complicity in the conspiracy of Piso, he committed suicide in obedience to Nero's order; his extant writings are numerous, and include "Benefits," "Clemency," and "Minor Essays." [1]

I

OF THE WISE MAN

I MIGHT truly say, Serenus, that there is as wide a difference between the Stoics and the other sects of philosophers as there is between men and women, since each class contributes an equal share to human society, but the one is born to command, the other to obey. The other

---

[1] Seneca's influence on writers in his own day was notable. He seems almost to have superseded Cicero as a model. Critics of our day, while recognizing all this and the charm of his style, have found in his philosophy a lack of sincere qualities. An old question is that of his relations to Christianity. So much in his writings partakes of the spirit of the Apostles that he has been credited with having been influenced by them. It is known that his brother Gallio met St. Paul in Corinth and that Burrus, the colleague and intimate friend of Seneca, was the captain of the Prætorian guards before whom St. Paul was brought in Rome. Cruttwell dismisses the claim, believing that Seneca's philos-

philosophers deal with us gently and coaxingly, just as our accustomed family physicians usually do with our bodies, treating them not by the best and shortest method, but by that which we allow them to employ; whereas the Stoics adopt a manly course, and do not care about its appearing attractive to those who are entering upon it, but that it should as quickly as possible take us out of the world, and lead us to that lofty eminence which is so far beyond the scope of any missile weapon that it is above the reach of Fortune herself. "But the way by which we are asked to climb is steep and uneven." What then? Can heights be reached by a level path? Yet they are not so sheer and precipitous as some think. It is only the first part that has rocks and cliffs and no apparent outlet, just as many hills seen from a long way off appear abruptly steep and joined together, because the distance deceives our sight, and then, as we draw nearer, those very hills which our mistaken eyes had made into one gradually unfold themselves, those parts which seemed precipitous from afar assume a gently sloping outline. When just now mention was made of Marcus Cato, you whose mind revolts at injustice were indignant at Cato's own age having so little understood him, at its having allotted a place below Vatinius to one who tow-

ophy was "the natural development of the thoughts of his predecessors in a mind at once capacious and smitten with the love of virtue." Philosophy to Seneca was "altogether a question of practise." Like other thinkers of his day, "he cared nothing for consistency of opinion, everything for impressiveness of application."

² From Book II of the "Minor Essays." Translated by Aubrey Stewart.

ered above both Cæsar and Pompey; it seemed shameful to you, that when he spoke against some law in the Forum his toga was torn from him, and that he was hustled through the hands of a mutinous mob from the Rostra as far as the arch of Fabius,[3] enduring all the bad language, spitting, and other insults of the frantic rabble.

I then answered, that you had good cause to be anxious on behalf of the commonwealth, which Publius Clodius on the one side, Vatinius and all the greatest scoundrels on the other, were putting up for sale, and, carried away by their blind covetousness, did not understand that when they sold it they themselves were sold with it; I bade you have no fears on behalf of Cato himself, because the wise man can neither receive injury nor insult, and it is more certain that the immortal gods have given Cato as a pattern of a wise man to us, than that they gave Ulysses or Hercules to the earlier ages; for these our Stoics have declared were wise men, unconquered by labors, despisers of pleasure, and superior to all terrors. Cato did not slay wild beasts, whose pursuit belongs to huntsmen and countrymen, nor did he exterminate fabulous creatures with fire and sword, or live in times when it was possible to believe that the heavens could be supported on the shoulders of one man. In an age which had thrown off its belief in antiquated superstitions, and had carried material knowledge to its highest point, he had to struggle against

[3] Quintilius Fabius, the general, who before the battle of Cannæ commanded in Italy against Hannibal. He was famous for avoiding pitched battles and hence the term "Fabian policy."

that many-headed monster, ambition, against that boundless lust for power which the whole world divided among three men could not satisfy. He alone withstood the vices of a worn-out state sinking into ruin through its own bulk; he upheld the falling commonwealth as far as it could be upheld by one man's hand, until at last his support was withdrawn, and he shared the crash which he had so long averted, and perished together with that from which it was impious to separate him—for Cato did not outlive freedom, nor did freedom outlive Cato. Think you that the people could do any wrong to such a man when they tore away his prætorship or his toga? when they bespattered his sacred head with the rinsings of their mouths? The wise man is safe, and no injury or insult can touch him. . . .

Consider now, whether any thief, or false accuser, or headstrong neighbor, or rich man enjoying the power conferred by a childless old age, could do any injury to this man, from whom neither war nor an enemy whose profession was the noble art of battering city walls could take away anything. Amid the flash of swords on all sides, and the riot of the plundering soldiery, amid the flames and blood and ruin of the fallen city, amid the crash of temples falling upon their gods, one man was at peace. You need not therefore account that a reckless boast, for which I will give you a surety, if my word goes for nothing. Indeed, you would hardly believe so much constancy or such greatness of mind to belong to any man; but here a man comes forward to prove that you have no reason for doubting that one who is but of human birth can raise himself above human necessities, can tranquilly behold pains, losses, diseases, wounds, and great natural convulsions roaring around him, can bear adversity with calm and prosperity with moderation, neither yielding to the former nor trusting to the latter, that he can remain the same amid all varieties of fortune, and think nothing to be his own save himself, and himself too only as regards his better part. . . .

You have no cause for saying, as you are wont to do, that this wise man of ours is nowhere to be found; we do not invent him as an unreal glory of the human race, or conceive a mighty shadow of an untruth, but we have displayed and will display him just as we sketch him, tho he may perhaps be uncommon, and only one appears at long intervals; for what is great and transcends the common ordinary type is not often produced; but this very Marcus Cato himself, the mention of whom started this discussion, was a man who I fancy even surpassed our model. Moreover, that which hurts must be stronger than that which is hurt. Now wickedness is not stronger than virtue; therefore the wise man can not be hurt. Only the bad attempt to injure the good. Good men are at peace among themselves; bad ones are equally mischievous to the good and to one another. If a man can not be hurt by one weaker than himself, and a bad man be weaker than a good one, and the good have no injury to dread, except from one unlike themselves; then, no injury takes effect upon the wise man; for by this time I need not remind you that no one save the wise man is good. . . .

The nobler a man is by birth, by reputation,

SENECA

or by inheritance, the more bravely he should bear himself, remembering that the tallest men stand in the front rank in battle. As for insults, offensive language, marks of disgrace, and such like disfigurements, he ought to bear them as he would bear the shouts of the enemy, and darts or stones flung from a distance, which rattle upon his helmet without causing a wound; while he should look upon injuries as wounds, some received on his armor and others on his body, which he endures without falling or even leaving his place in the ranks. Even tho you be hard prest and violently attacked by the enemy, still it is base to give way; hold the post assigned to you by nature. You ask, what this post is? it is that of being a man. The wise man has another help, of the opposite kind to this; you are hard at work, while he has already won the victory. Do not quarrel with your own good advantage, and, until you shall have made your way to the truth, keep alive this hope in your minds, be willing to receive the news of a better life, and encourage it by your admiration and your prayers; it is to the interest of the commonwealth of mankind that there should be some one who is unconquered, some one against whom fortune has no power.

THE BEST OF THE WORLD'S CLASSICS

II

OF CONSOLATION FOR THE LOSS OF FRIENDS[4]

Why should I lead you on through the endless series of great men and pick out the unhappy ones, as tho it were not more difficult to find happy ones? for how few households have remained possest of all their members to the end? what one is there that has not suffered some loss? Take any one year you please and name the Consuls for it; if you like, that of Lucius Bibulus[5] and Julius Cæsar; you will see that, tho these colleagues were each other's bitterest enemies, yet their fortunes agreed. Lucius Bibulus, a man more remarkable for goodness than for strength of character, had both his sons murdered at the same time, and even insulted by the Egyptian soldiery, so that the agent of his bereavement was as much a subject for tears as the bereavement itself. Nevertheless Bibulus, who during the whole of his year of office had remained hidden in his house, to cast reproach upon his colleague Cæsar on the day following that upon which he heard of both his sons' deaths, came forth and went through the routine business of

[4] From Book VI of the "Minor Essays." Translated by Aubrey Stewart. Marcia, to whom this letter was addrest, was "a respectable and opulent lady," the daughter of Cremutius Cordus.

[5] Made Consul with Julius Cæsar in 59 B.C. He represented the aristocratic party and bitterly opposed some of the measures of Cæsar. In the war with Pompey he joined his forces to those of Pompey.

134

his magistracy. Who could devote less than one day to mourning for two sons? Thus soon did he end his mourning for his children, altho he had mourned a whole year for his consulship. Gaius Cæsar, after having traversed Britain, and not allowed even the ocean to set bounds to his successes, heard of the death of his daughter, which hurried on the crisis of affairs. Already Cnæus Pompey stood before his eyes, a man who would ill endure that any one besides himself should become a great power in the state, and one who was likely to place a check upon his advancement, which he had regarded as onerous even when each gained by the other's rise: yet within three days' time he resumed his duties as general, and conquered his grief as quickly as he was wont to conquer everything else.

Why need I remind you of the deaths of the other Cæsars, whom fortune appears to me sometimes to have outraged in order that even by their deaths they might be useful to mankind, by proving that not even they, altho they were styled "sons of gods," and "fathers of gods to come," could exercise the same power over their own fortunes which they did over those of others? The Emperor Augustus lost his children and his grandchildren, and after all the family of Cæsar had perished was obliged to prop his empty house by adopting a son: yet he bore his losses as bravely as tho he were already personally concerned in the honor of the gods, and as tho it were especially to his interest that no one should complain of the injustice of Heaven. Tiberius Cæsar lost both the son whom he begot and the son whom he adopted, yet he himself pronounced a panegyric upon his son from the Rostra, and stood in full view of the corpse, which merely had a curtain on one side to prevent the eyes of the high priest resting upon the dead body, and did not change his countenance, tho all the Romans wept: he gave Sejanus, who stood by his side, a proof of how patiently he could endure the loss of his relatives. See you not what numbers of most eminent men there have been, none of whom have been spared by this blight which prostrates us all: men, too, adorned with every grace of character, and every distinction that public or private life can confer. It appears as tho this plague moved in a regular orbit, and spread ruin and desolation among us all without distinction of persons, all being alike its prey. Bid any number of individuals tell you the story of their lives: you will find that all have paid some penalty for being born.

I know what you will say, "You quote men as examples: you forget that it is a woman that you are trying to console." Yet who would say that nature has dealt grudgingly with the minds of women and stunted their virtues? Believe me, they have the same intellectual power as men, and the same capacity for honorable and generous action. If trained to do so, they are just as able to endure sorrow or labor. Ye good gods, do I say this in that very city in which Lucretia and Brutus removed the yoke of kings from the necks of the Romans? We owe liberty to Brutus, but we owe Brutus to Lucretia—in which Clœlia,[6]

---

[6] A legendary maiden delivered as hostage to Lars Porsena of Clusium, but who escaped by swimming across the Tiber.

for the sublime courage with which she scorned both the enemy and the river, has been almost reckoned as a man.

The statue of Clœlia, mounted on horseback, in that busiest of thoroughfares, the Sacred Way, continually reproaches the youth of the present day, who never mount anything but a cushioned seat in a carriage, with journeying in such a fashion through that very city in which we have enrolled even women among our knights. If you wish me to point out to you examples of women who have bravely endured the loss of their children, I shall not go far afield to search for them: in one family I can quote two Cornelias, one the daughter of Scipio, and the mother of Gracchi, who made acknowledgment of the birth of her twelve children by burying them all; nor was it so hard to do this in the case of the others, whose birth and death were alike unknown to the public, but she beheld the murdered and unburied corpses of both Tiberius Gracchus and Gaius Gracchus, whom even those who will not call them good must admit were great men. Yet to those who tried to console her and called her unfortunate, she answered, "I shall never cease to call myself happy, because I am the mother of the Gracchi." Cornelia, the wife of Livius Drusus,[7] lost by the hands of an unknown assassin a young son of great distinction, who was treading in the footsteps of the Gracchi, and was murdered in his own house just when he had

---

[7] Marcus Livius Drusus was a politician, who in 91 B.C. became tribune of the plebs. He was about to bring forward a proposal giving citizenship to Italians when he was assassinated, an event which precipitated the Social War.

so many bills half-way through the process of becoming law: nevertheless she bore the untimely and unavenged death of her son with as lofty a spirit as he had shown in carrying his laws.

Will you not, Marcia, forgive fortune because she has not refrained from striking you with the darts which she launched at the Scipios, and the mothers and daughters of the Scipios, and with which she has attacked the Cæsars themselves? Life is full of misfortunes; our path is beset with them: no one can make a long peace, nay, scarcely an armistice with fortune. You, Marcia, have borne four children; now they say that no dart which is hurled into a close column of soldiers can fail to hit one—ought you then to wonder at not having been able to lead along such a company without exciting the ill-will of Fortune, or suffering loss at her hands? . . .

Think how great a blessing is a timely death, how many have been injured by living longer than they ought. If sickness had carried off that glory and support of the empire, Cnæus Pompey, at Naples, he would have died undoubted head of the Roman people, but as it was, a short extension of time cast him down from his pinnacle of fame: he beheld his legions slaughtered before his eyes: and what a sad relic of that battle, in which the Senate formed the first line, was the survival of the general. He saw his Egyptian butcher, and offered his body, hallowed by so many victories, to a guardsman's sword, altho even had he been unhurt, he would have regretted his safety: for what could have been more infamous than that a Pompey should owe his life to the clemency of a king? If Marcus Cicero had fallen at the time when he avoided those dangers which Catiline aimed equally at him and at his country, he might have died as the savior of the commonwealth which he had set free: if his death had even followed upon that of his daughter, he might have died happy. He would not then have seen swords drawn for the slaughter of Roman citizens, the goods of the murdered divided among the murderers, that men might pay from their own purse the price of their own blood, the public auction of the Consul's spoil in the civil war, the public letting out of murder to be done, brigandage, war, pillage, hosts of Catilines. Would it not have been a good thing for Marcus Cato if the sea had swallowed him up when he was returning from Cyprus after sequestrating the king's hereditary possessions, even if that very money which he was bringing to pay the soldiers in the civil war had been lost with him? He certainly would have been able to boast that no one would dare to do wrong in the presence of Cato: as it was, the extension of his life for a very few more years forced one who was born for personal and political freedom to flee from Cæsar and to become Pompey's follower. Premature death therefore did him no evil: indeed, it put an end to the power of any evil to hurt him. . . .

Born for a very brief space of time, we regard this life as an inn which we are soon to quit that it may be made ready for the coming guest. Do I speak of our lives, which we know roll away incredibly fast? Reckon up the centuries of cities: you will find that even those which boast of their antiquity have not existed for long. All human works are brief and fleeting: they take up no part whatever of infinite time. Tried by the standard of the universe, we regard this earth of ours, with all its cities, nations, rivers, and seaboard, as a mere point: our life occupies less than a point when compared with all time, the measure of which exceeds that of the world, for indeed the world is contained many times in it. Of what importance, then, can it be to lengthen that which, however much you add to it, will never be much more than nothing? We can only make our lives long by one expedient, that is, by being satisfied with their length: you may tell me of long-lived men, whose length of days has been celebrated by tradition, you may assign a hundred and ten years apiece to them: yet when you allow your mind to conceive the idea of eternity, there will be no difference between the shortest and the longest life, if you compare the time during which any one has been alive with that during which he has not been alive. In the next place, when he died his life was complete: he had lived as long as he needed to live: there was nothing left for him to accomplish.

III

TO NERO ON CLEMENCY[*]

You, Cæsar, can boldly say that everything which has come into your charge has been kept safe, and that the state has neither openly nor secretly suffered any loss at your hands. You have coveted a glory which is most rare, and which has been obtained by no emperor before you, that of innocence. Your remarkable goodness is not thrown away, nor is it ungratefully or spitefully undervalued. Men feel gratitude toward you: no one person ever was so dear to another as you are to the people of Rome, whose great and enduring benefit you are. You have, however, taken upon yourself a mighty burden: no one any longer speaks of the good times of the late Emperor Augustus, or the first years of the reign of Tiberius, or proposes for your imitation any model outside yourself: yours is a pattern reign. This would have been difficult had your goodness of heart not been innate, but merely adopted for a time; for no one can wear a mask for long, and fictitious qualities soon give place to true ones. Those which are founded upon truth, become greater and better as time goes on.

[*] From the "Minor Essays." Translated by Aubrey Stewart. "This," says Alexander Thomson, the eighteenth-century translator of Suetonius, "appears to have been written in the beginning of the reign of Nero, on whom the author bestows some high encomiums which at that time seem not to have been destitute of foundation."

The Roman people were in a state of great hazard as long as it was uncertain how your generous disposition would turn out: now, however, the prayers of the community are sure of an answer, for there is no fear that you should suddenly forget your own character. Indeed, excess of happiness makes men greedy, and our desires are never so moderate as to be bounded by what they have obtained: great successes become the stepping-stones to greater ones, and those who have obtained more than they hoped, entertain even more extravagant hopes than before; yet by all your countrymen we hear it admitted that they are now happy, and moreover, that nothing can be added to the blessings that they enjoy, except that they should be eternal. Many circumstances force this admission from them, altho it is the one which men are least willing to make: we enjoy a profound and prosperous peace, the power of the law has been openly asserted in the sight of all men, and raised beyond the reach of any violent interference: the form of our government is so happy, as to contain all the essentials of liberty except the power of destroying itself. It is nevertheless your clemency which is most especially admired by the high and low alike: every man enjoys or hopes to enjoy the other blessings of your rule according to the measure of his own personal good fortune, whereas from your clemency all hope alike: no one has so much confidence in his innocence, as not to feel glad that in your presence stands a clemency which is ready to make allowance for human errors. . . .

Since I have made mention of the gods, I shall

state the best model on which a prince may mold his life to be, that he deal with his countrymen as he would that the gods may deal with himself. Is it then desirable that the gods should show no mercy upon sins and mistakes, and that they should harshly pursue us to our ruin? In that case what king will be safe? Whose limbs will not be torn asunder and collected by the soothsayers? If, on the other hand, the gods are placable and kind, and do not at once avenge the crimes of the powerful with thunderbolts, is it not far more just that a man set in authority over other men should exercise his power in a spirit of clemency and should consider whether the condition of the world is more beauteous and pleasant to the eyes on a fine calm day, or when everything is shaken with frequent thunder-claps and when lightning flashes on all sides! Yet the appearance of a peaceful and constitutional reign is the same as that of the calm and brilliant sky. A cruel reign is disordered and hidden in darkness, and while all shake with terror at the sudden explosions, not even he who caused all this disturbance escapes unharmed. It is easier to find excuses for private men who obstinately claim their rights; possibly they may have been injured and their rage may spring from their wrongs; besides this, they fear to be despised, and not to return the injuries which they have received looks like weakness rather than clemency; but one who can easily avenge himself, if he neglects to do so, is certain to gain praise for goodness of heart. Those who are born in a humble station may with greater freedom exercise violence, go to law, engage in quarrels, and indulge their angry passions; even blows count for little between two equals; but in case of a king, even loud clamor and unmeasured talk are unbecoming. . . .

Such was Augustus when an old man, or when growing old: in his youth he was hasty and passionate, and did many things upon which he looked back with regret. No one will venture to compare the rule of the blest Augustus to the mildness of your own, even if your youth be compared with his more than ripe old age: he was gentle and placable, but it was after he had dyed the sea at Actium with Roman blood; after he had wrecked both the enemy's fleet and his own at Sicily; after the holocaust of Perusia and the proscriptions. But I do not call it clemency to be wearied of cruelty; true clemency, Cæsar, is that which you display, which has not begun from remorse at its past ferocity, on which there is no stain, which has never shed the blood of your countrymen: this, when combined with unlimited power, shows the truest self-control and all-embracing love of the human race as of one's self, not corrupted by any low desires, any extravagant ideas, or any of the bad examples of former emperors into trying, by actual experiment, how great a tyranny you would be allowed to exercise over his countrymen, but inclining rather to blunting your sword of empire.

You, Cæsar, have granted us the boon of keeping our state free from bloodshed, and that of which you boast, that you have not caused one single drop of blood to flow in any part of the world, is all the more magnanimous and marvelous because no one ever had the power of the

SENECA

sword placed in his hands at an earlier age. Clemency, then, makes empires besides being their most trustworthy means of preservation. Why have legitimate sovereigns grown old on the throne, and bequeathed their power to their children and grandchildren, while the sway of despotic usurpers is both hateful and short-lived? What is the difference between the tyrant and the king—for their outward symbols of authority and their powers are the same—except it be that tyrants take delight in cruelty, whereas kings are only cruel for good reasons and because they can not help it. . . .

Nothing can be imagined which is more becoming to a sovereign than clemency, by whatever title and right he may be set over his fellow citizens. The greater his power, the more beautiful and admirable he will confess his clemency to be: for there is no reason why power should do any harm, if only it be wielded in accordance with the laws of nature. Nature herself has conceived the idea of a king, as you may learn from various animals, and especially from bees, among whom the king's cell is the roomiest, and is placed in the most central and safest part of the hive; moreover, he does no work, but employs himself in keeping the others up to their work. If the king be lost, the entire swarm disperses: they never endure to have more than one king at a time, and find out which is the better by making them fight with one another: moreover the king is distinguished by his statelier appearance, being both larger and more brilliantly colored than the other bees.

The most remarkable distinction, however, is

the following: bees are very fierce, and for their size are the most pugnacious of creatures, and leave their stings in the wounds which they make, but the king himself has no sting: nature does not wish him to be savage or to seek revenge at so dear a rate, and so has deprived him of his weapon and disarmed his rage. She has offered him as a pattern to great sovereigns; for she is wont to practise herself in small matters, and to scatter abroad tiny models of the hugest structures. We ought to be ashamed of not learning a lesson in behavior from these small creatures, for a man, who has so much more power of doing harm than they, ought to show a correspondingly greater amount of self-control. Would that human beings were subject to the same law, and that their anger destroyed itself together with its instruments, so that they could only inflict a wound once, and would not make use of the strength of others to carry out their hatreds; for their fury would soon grow faint if it carried its own punishment with it, and could only give rein to its violence at the risk of death. Even as it is, however, no one can exercise it with safety, for he must needs feel as much fear as he hopes to cause, he must watch every one's movements, and even when his enemies are not laying violent hands upon him he must bear in mind that they are plotting to do so, and he can not have a single moment free from alarm. Would any one endure to live such a life as this, when he might enjoy all the privileges of his high station to the general joy of all men, without fear? for it is a mistake to suppose that the king can be safe in a state where nothing is safe from the king: he can only purchase a life without anxiety for himself by guaranteeing the same for his subjects. He need not pile up lofty citadels, escarp steep hills, cut away the sides of mountains, and fence himself about with many lines of walls and towers: clemency will render a king safe even upon an open plain. The one fortification which can not be stormed is the love of his countrymen. . . .

The reason why cruelty is the most hateful of all vices is that it goes first beyond ordinary limits, and then beyond those of humanity; that it devises new kinds of punishments, calls ingenuity to aid it in inventing devices for varying and lengthening men's torture, and takes delight in their sufferings: this accursed disease of the mind reaches its highest pitch of madness when cruelty itself turns into pleasure and the act of killing a man becomes enjoyment. Such a ruler is soon cast down from his throne; his life is attempted by poison one day and by the sword the next; he is exposed to as many dangers as there are men to whom he is dangerous, and he is sometimes destroyed by the plots of individuals, and at others by a general insurrection. Whole communities are not roused to action by unimportant outrages on private persons; but cruelty which takes a wider range, and from which no one is safe, becomes a mark for all men's weapons. Very small snakes escape our notice, and the whole country does not combine to destroy them; but when one of them exceeds the usual size and grows into a monster, when it poisons fountains with its spittle, scorches herbage with its breath, and spreads ruin wherever it crawls, we shoot at it with military engines. Trifling evils may cheat us and elude our observation, but we gird up our loins to attack great ones. One sick person does not so much as disquiet the house in which he lies; but when frequent deaths show that a plague is raging, there is a general outcry, men take to flight and shake their fists angrily at the very gods themselves. If a fire breaks out under one single roof, the family and the neighbors pour water upon it; but a wide conflagration which has consumed many houses must be smothered under the ruins of a whole quarter of a city. . . .

I have been especially led to write about clemency, Nero Cæsar, by a saying of yours, which I remember having heard with admiration and which I afterward told to others: a noble saying, showing a great mind and great gentleness, which suddenly burst from you without premeditation, and was not meant to reach any ears but your own, and which displayed the conflict which was raging between your natural goodness and your imperial duties. Your præfect Burrus,[9] an excellent man who was born to be the servant of such an emperor as you are, was about to order two brigands to be executed, and was pressing you to write their names and the grounds on which they were to be put to death; this had often been put off, and he was insisting that it

---

[9] Barrus in 52 A.D. had been made sole Prætorian Præfect by Claudius and, conjointly with Seneca, was entrusted with the education of Nero. It was his influence with the Prætorian Guards that secured to Nero in 54 the independent succession. He was put to death by poison, under orders from Nero, who had been offended by the severity of his moral conduct.

should then be done. When he reluctantly produced the document and put it in your equally reluctant hands, you exclaimed: "Would that I had never learned my letters!" O what a speech, how worthy to be heard by all nations, both those who dwell within the Roman Empire, those who enjoy a debatable independence upon its borders, and those who either in will or in deed fight against it! It is a speech which ought to be spoken before a meeting of all mankind, whose words all kings and princes ought to swear to and obey: a speech worthy of the days of human innocence, and worthy to bring back that golden age. Now in truth we ought all to agree to love righteousness and goodness, covetousness, which is the root of all evil, ought to be driven away, piety and virtue, good faith and modesty ought to resume their interrupted reign, and the vices which have so long and so shamefully ruled us ought at last to give way to an age of happiness and purity.

IV

THE PILOT [19]

A tempest and storme hurt a Pilot, but notwithstanding they make him not worse. Certaine Stoicks do thus answer against this, that a Pilot is made worse by a tempest and by a storme, because that thing which he had purposed he

[19] From Epistle 85. Translated by Thomas Lodge. Printed here with the spelling and punctuation of the first edition (1613).

cannot effect, nor keep on his course. Worse is he made, not in his skill, but in his work. To whom the Aristotelian: therefore, saith he, pouertie and dolour, and what soeuer such like thing there shall be, shall not take vertue from him, but shall hinder his working thereof.

This were rightly said, except the condition of a Pilot and of a wise-man were unlike. For the purpose of him is in leading his life, not without faile to effect that which he assayeth to doe, but to doe all things aright. It is the purpose of the Pilot, without faile to bring a ship into a hauen. They be seruile arts, they ought to performe that which they promise. Wisedome is mistresse and gouernesse. The arts doe serue to, wisedome commandeth our life. I judge that we must answere after another sort, namely that neyther the skill of the gouernour is made worse by any tempest, nor yet the very administration of art. The gouernour hath not promised prosperous successe unto thee, but his profitable endeuour, and skill to gouerne the ship. This appeareth the more, by how much the more some force of fortune hath hindered him. He that hath beene able to say this, O Neptune, this ship was neuer but right, hath satisfied skill. A tempest hindereth not the work of a pilot, but the successe.

What therefore sayeth thou? Doth not that thing hurt a Pilot, which hindereth him from entring the Port? Which causeth his endeuours to be vaine? Which eyther beareth him back, or detaineth and disarmeth him? It hurteth him not as Pilot, but as one that doth saile. Otherwise it doth not so much hinder, as shew the Pilot's skill. For euery one can, as they say, be a pilot in the calme. These things hinder the ship; not a pilot as he is a pilot. Two persons a pilot hath; the one common with all who haue gone aboard the same ship, wherein he himselfe also is a passenger; the other proper as he is gouernour. The tempest hurteth him as he is a passenger not as a Pilot. Furthermore the art of a Pilot is another good, it apperteineth to those whom he carrieth: as the art of a Physitian apperteineth to those whom he doth cure. Wisedome is a common good; and is proper to ownes selfe, for those with whom he doth liue. Therefore peraduenture a Pilot is hurt, whose promised seruice to others is let by a tempest.

A wise man is not hurt by pouertie, nor by doulour, nor by other tempests of life. For not all workes of him be hindered, but only those that pertain to other men; always is he himself indeed, the greatest of all, when fortune hath opposed herselfe unto him, then manageth he the businesse of wisdome itselfe: which wisdome we haue said to be both anothers and his owne good. Furthermore not then indeed is he hindered to profite other men, when some necessities do presse him. Through pouertie he is hindred to teach, how a Commonwealth may be managed: but he teacheth that thing, how pouertie is to be managed. His worke is extended all his life long. Thus no fortune, no thing excludeth the acts of a wise-man. For he doth not that verie thing, whereby he is forbidden to do other things. He is fit for both chances: a gouernour of the bad, an ouercommer of the good. So I say hath he exercised himselfe, that he sheweth vertue as well in prosperous as in aduerse affaires; neyther looketh he upon the matter thereof, but upon itselfe. Therefore neither pouerty nor doulour, nor any other thing which turneth back the unskilfull, and driuest them headlong, hindereth them. Hast thou rather he should be pressed? He maketh use of it. Not only of iuorie did Phidias know how to make images: he made them of brasse. If marble were unto him, if thou hadst offered baser matter, he would haue made such a one thereof, as could be made of that which was the best.

So a wise-man will show uertue, if he may, in wealth, if not in pouertie: if he shall be able, in his countrie; if not in banishment: if he can, being a commander; if not, being a souldier: if he can being sound; if not, being weake: what fortune soeuer he shall entertaine, he will performe some memorable thing thereby. Certain tamers there be of wild beasts, who teach the fiercest creatures, and which terrifie a man when they meet him, to suffer the yoake: and not wanted to have shaken fiercenesse off, do tame them, euer to keep them companie. The master useth often to thrust out his hand to Lions; they kisse it. The keeper commandeth his tyger; the Æthiopian Player commandeth his elephants to fall upon their knees, and to walke upon a rope. so a wise-man is skilfull to subdue euil things. Dolour, pouertie, ignominie, prison, banishment, when they come unto him, are made tame.

SENECA

V

OF A HAPPY LIFE [11]

ALL men, brother Gallio, wish to live happily, but are dull at perceiving exactly what it is that makes life happy: and so far is it from being easy to attain to happiness that the more eagerly a man struggles to reach it the further he departs from it, if he takes the wrong road; for, since this leads in the opposite direction, his very swiftness carries him all the further away. We must therefore first define clearly what it is at which we aim: next we must consider by what path we may most speedily reach it, for on our journey itself, provided it be made in the right direction, we shall learn how much progress we have made each day, and how much nearer we are to the goal toward which our natural desires urge us. But as long as we wander at random, not following any guide except the shouts and discordant clamors of those who invite us to proceed in different directions, our short life will be wasted in useless roamings, even if we labor both day and night to get a good understanding. Let us not therefore decide whither we must tend, and by what path, without the advice of some experienced person who has explored the region which we are about to enter, because this

[11] From Book VII of the "Minor Essays." Translated by Aubrey Stewart. This essay address to Gallio, Seneca is thought to have intended "as a vindication of himself against those who calumniated him on account of his riches and manner of living."

journey is not subject to the same conditions as others; for in them some distinctly understood track and inquiries made of the natives make it impossible for us to go wrong, but here the most beaten and frequented tracks are those which lead us astray. Nothing, therefore, is more important than that we should not, like sheep, follow the flock that has gone before us, and thus proceed not whither we ought, but whither the rest are going. . . .

True wisdom consists in not departing from nature and in molding our conduct according to her laws and model. A happy life, therefore, is one which is in accordance with its own nature, and can not be brought about unless in the first place the mind be sound and vigorous, enduring all things with most admirable courage suited to the times in which it lives, careful of the body and its appurtenances, yet not troublesomely careful. It must also set due value upon all the things which adorn our lives, without overestimating any one of them, and must be able to enjoy the bounty of Fortune without becoming her slave. . . .

A happy life consists in a mind which is free, upright, undaunted, and stedfast beyond the influence of fear or desire, which thinks nothing good except honor, and nothing bad except shame, and regards everything else as a mass of mean details which can neither add anything to nor take anything away from the happiness of life, but which come and go without either increasing or diminishing the highest good? A man of these principles, whether he will or no, must be accompanied by a continual cheerfulness, a high happiness, which comes indeed from on high because he delights in what he has, and desires no greater pleasures than those which his home affords. Is he not right in allowing these to turn the scale against petty, ridiculous, and short-lived movements of his wretched body? on the day on which he becomes proof against pleasure he also becomes proof against pain. See, on the other hand, how evil and guilty a slavery a man is forced to serve who is dominated in turn by pleasures and pains, those most untrustworthy and passionate of masters. We must, therefore, escape from them into freedom. This nothing will bestow upon us save contempt of Fortune; but if we attain to this, then there will dawn upon us those invaluable blessings, the repose of a mind that is at rest in a safe haven, its lofty imaginings, its great and steady delight at casting out errors and learning to know the truth, its courtesy and its cheerfulness, in all of which we shall take delight, not regarding them as good things, but as proceeding from the proper good of man. . . .

Why do you put together two things which are unlike and even incompatible one with another? virtue is a lofty quality, sublime, royal, unconquerable, untiring: pleasure is low, slavish, weakly, perishable; its haunts and homes are the brothel and the tavern. You will meet virtue in the temple, the market-place, the senate-house, manning the walls, covered with dust, sunburnt, horny-handed: you will find pleasure skulking out of sight, seeking for shady nooks at the public baths, hot chambers, and places which dread the visits of the ædile, soft, effeminate, reeking of wine and perfumes, pale or perhaps painted and made up with cosmetics. The highest good is immortal: it knows no ending, and does not admit of either satiety or regret: for a right-thinking mind never alters or becomes hateful to itself, nor do the best things ever undergo any change: but pleasure dies at the very moment when it charms us most: it has no great scope, and therefore it soon cloys and wearies us, and fades away as soon as its first impulse is over: indeed, we can not depend upon anything whose nature is to change. Consequently, it is not even possible that there should be any solid substance in that which comes and goes so swiftly and which perishes by the very exercise of its own functions, for it arrives at a point at which it ceases to be, and even while it is beginning always keeps its end in view. . . .

A man should be unbiassed and not to be conquered by external things: he ought to admire himself alone, to feel confidence in his own spirit, and so to order his life as to be ready alike for good or bad fortune. Let not his confidence be without knowledge, nor his knowledge without stedfastness: let him always abide by what he has once determined, and let there be no erasure in his doctrine. It will be understood, even tho I append it not, that such a man will be tranquil and composed in his demeanor, high-minded and courteous in his actions. Let reason be encouraged by the senses to seek for the truth, and draw its first principles from thence: indeed it has no other base of operations or place from which to start in pursuit of truth: it must fall back upon itself. Even the all-embracing universe and God who is its guide extends Himself forth into outward things, and yet altogether returns from all sides back to Himself. Let our mind do the same thing: when, following its bodily senses, it has by means of them sent itself forth into the things of the outward world, let it remain still their master and its own. By this means we shall obtain a strength and an ability which are united and allied together; we shall derive from it that reason which never halts between two opinions, nor is dull in forming its perceptions, beliefs, or convictions. Such a mind, when it has ranged itself in order, made its various parts agree together, and, if I may so express myself, harmonized them, has attained to the highest good: for it has nothing evil or hazardous remaining, nothing to shake it or make it stumble: it will do everything under the guidance of its own will, and nothing unexpected will befall it, but whatever may be done by it will turn out well, and that, too, readily and easily, without the doer having recourse to any underhand devices: for slow and hesitating purpose. You may, then, boldly declare that the highest good is singleness of mind: for where agreement and unity are, there must the virtues be: it is the vices that are at war with one another. . . .

It is the act of the generous spirit to proportion its efforts not to its own strength, but to that of human nature, to entertain lofty aims, and to conceive plans which are too vast to be carried into execution even by those who are endowed with gigantic intellects, who appoint for themselves the following rules: "I will look upon death or upon a comedy with the same expression of countenance: I will submit to labors, however great they may be, supporting the strength of my body by that of my mind: I will despise riches when I have them as much as when I have them not; if they be elsewhere I will not be more gloomy, if they sparkle around me I will not be more lively than I should otherwise be: whether Fortune comes or goes I will take no notice of her: I will view all lands as tho they belonged to me, and my own as tho they belonged to all mankind: I will so live as to remember that I was born for others, and will thank Nature on this account: for in what fashion could she have done better for me? she has given me alone to all, and all to me alone. Whatever I may possess, I will neither hoard it greedily nor squander it recklessly. I will think that I have no possessions so real as those which I have given away to deserving people: I will not reckon benefits by their magnitude or number, or by anything except the value set upon them by the receiver: I never will consider a gift to be a large one if it be bestowed upon a worthy object. I will do nothing because of public opinion, but everything because of conscience: whenever I do anything alone by myself I will believe that the eyes of the Roman people are upon me while I do it. In eating and drinking my object shall be to quench the desires of Nature, not to fill and empty my belly. I will be agreeable with my friends, gentle and mild to my foes: I will grant pardon before I am asked for it, and will meet the wishes of honorable men half-way. I will bear in mind that the world is my native city, that its governors are the gods, and that they stand above and around me, criticizing whatever I do or say. Whenever either Nature demands my breath again, or reason bids me dismiss it, I will quit this life, calling all to witness that I have loved a good conscience, and good pursuits; that no one's freedom, my own least of all, has been impaired through me.'' He who sets up these as the rules of his life will soar aloft and strive to make his way to the gods: of a truth, even tho he fails, yet he

"Fails in a high emprise."

But you, who hate both virtue and those who practise it, do nothing at which we need be surprised, for sickly lights can not bear the sun, nocturnal creatures avoid the brightness of day, and at its first dawning become bewildered and all betake themselves to their dens together: creatures that fear the light hide themselves in crevices. So croak away, and exercise your miserable tongues in reproaching good men: open wide your jaws, bite hard: you will break many teeth before you make any impression. . . .

Where, indeed, can fortune invest riches more securely than in a place from whence they can always be recovered without any squabble with their trustee? Marcus Cato, when he was praising Curius and Coruncanius and that century in which the possession of a few small silver coins were an offense which was punished by the Censor, himself owned four million sesterces; a less fortune, no doubt, than that of Crassus, but larger than of Cato the Censor. If the amounts be compared, he had outstript his great-grandfather further than he himself was outdone by

Crassus, and if still greater riches had fallen to his lot, he would not have spurned them, for the wise man does not think himself unworthy of any chance presents: he does not love riches, but he prefers to have them; he does not receive them into his spirit, but only into his house: nor does he cast away from him what he already possesses, but keeps them, and is willing that his virtue should receive a larger subject-matter for its exercise. . . .

Cease, then, forbidding philosophers to possess money: no one has condemned wisdom to poverty. The philosopher may own ample wealth, but will not own wealth that which has been torn from another, or which is stained with another's blood: his must be obtained without wronging any man, and without its being won by base means; it must be alike honorably come by and honorably spent, and must be such as spite could alone shake its head at. Raise it to whatever figure you please, it will still be an honorable possession, if, while it includes much which every man would like to call his own, there be nothing which any one can say is his own. Such a man will not forfeit his right to the favor of Fortune, and will neither boast of his inheritance nor blush for it if it was honorably acquired; yet he will have something to boast of, if he throw his house open, let all his countrymen come among his property, and say, "If any one recognizes here anything belonging to him, let him take it." What a great man, how excellently rich will he be, if after this speech he possesses as much as he had before! I say, then, that if he can safely and confidently submit his accounts to the scrutiny of the people, and no one can find in them any item upon which he can lay hands, such a man may boldly and unconcealedly enjoy his riches. The wise man will not allow a single ill-won penny to cross his threshold; yet he will not refuse or close his door against great riches, if they are the gift of fortune and the product of virtue: what reason has he for grudging them good quarters: let them come and be his guests: he will neither brag of them nor hide them away: the one is the part of a silly, the other of a cowardly and paltry spirit, which, as it were, muffles up a good thing in its lap. As he is capable of performing a journey upon his own feet, but yet would prefer to mount a carriage, just so he will be capable of being poor, yet will wish to be rich; he will own wealth, but will view it as an uncertain possession which will some day fly away from him. He will not allow it to be a burden either to himself or to any one else: he will give it—why do you prick up your ears? why do you open your pockets?— he will give it either to good men or to those whom it may make into good men. He will give it after having taken the utmost pains to choose those who are fittest to receive it, as becomes one who bears in mind that he ought to give an account of what he spends as well as of what he receives. He will give for good and commendable reasons, for a gift ill bestowed counts as a shameful loss: he will have an easily opened pocket, but not one with a hole in it, so that much may be taken out of it, yet nothing may fall out of it.

PLINY THE ELDER

Born in Como, in 23 A.D.; perished in the eruption of Vesuvius in 79; celebrated as naturalist; commanded cavalry in Germany at the age of twenty-three; procurator in Spain under Nero; wrote voluminously on military tactics, history, grammar and natural science; his death due to his efforts to observe more closely the eruption; of all his writings only his "Natural History" in thirty-seven books has survived.

I

THE QUALITIES OF THE DOG[1]

AMONG the animals that are domesticated with mankind there are many circumstances that are deserving of being known: among these there are more particularly that most faithful friend of man, the dog, and the horse. We have an account of a dog that fought against a band of robbers in defending its master; and altho it was pierced with wounds, still it would not leave the body, from which it drove away all birds and beasts. Another dog, in Epirus, recognized the murderer of its master in the midst of an assemblage of people, and, by biting and barking at him, extorted from him a confession of his crime. A king of the Garamantes,[2] also, was

[1] From the "Natural History." Translated by John Bostock and H. T. Riley.

[2] A name applied to tribes living in Africa east of the desert of Sahara.

162

PLINY THE ELDER

brought back from exile by two hundred dogs, which maintained the combat against all his opponents. The people of Colophon[3] and Castabala[4] kept troops of dogs for the purposes of war; and these used to fight in the front rank and never retreat; they were the most faithful of auxiliaries, and yet required no pay. After the defeat of the Cimbri[5] their dogs defended their movable houses, which were carried upon wagons. Jason, the Lycian, having been slain, his dog refused to take food, and died of famine. A dog, to which Darius gives the name of Hyrcanus, upon the funeral pile of King Lysimachus being lighted, threw itself into the flames; and the dog of King Hiero[6] did the same. Philistus also gives a similar account of Pyrrhus, the dog of the tyrant Gelon; and it is said also, that the dog of Nicomedes, King of Bithynia,[7] tore Consingis, the wife of that king, in consequence of her wanton behavior, when toying with her husband.

Dogs are the only animals that are sure to know their masters, and if they suddenly meet him as a stranger, they will instantly recognize him. They are the only animals that will answer to their names, and recognize the voices of the family. They recollect a road along which

[3] An Ionian city of Asia, distant seventy miles from Ephesus.

[4] An interior town of Cilicia, in Asia Minor.

[5] The home of this warlike people appears to have been Jutland.

[6] The tyrant king of Syracuse, successor to Gelon.

[7] A country of Asia Minor occupying a part of the Black Sea coast.

they have passed, however long it may be. Next to man there is no living creature whose memory is so retentive. By sitting down on the ground we may arrest their most impetuous attack, even when prompted by the most violent rage.

In daily life, we have discovered many other valuable qualities in this animal; but its intelligence and sagacity are more especially shown in the chase. It discovers and traces out the tracks of the animal, leading by the leash the sportsman who accompanies it straight up to the prey; and as soon as ever it has perceived it, how silent it is, and how secret but significant is the indication which it gives, first by the tail and afterward by the nose!

When Alexander the Great was on his Indian expedition, he was presented by the King of Albania with a dog of unusual size; being greatly delighted with its noble appearance, he ordered bears, and after them wild boars, and then deer, to be let loose before it; but the dog lay down and regarded them with a kind of immovable contempt. The noble spirit of the general became irritated by the sluggishness thus manifested by an animal of such vast bulk, and he ordered it to be killed. The report of this reached the king, who accordingly sent another dog, and at the same time sent word that its powers were to be tried, not upon small animals, but upon the lion or the elephant; adding, that he had originally but two, and that if this one were put to death, the race would be extinct. Alexander, without delay, procured a lion, which in his presence was instantly torn to pieces. He then ordered an elephant to be brought, and never was he more delighted with any spectacle; for the dog, bristling up its hair all over the body, began by thundering forth a loud barking, and then attacked the animal, leaping at it first on the one side and then on the other, attacking it in the most skilful manner, and then again retreating at the opportune moment, until at last the elephant, being rendered quite giddy by turning round and round, fell to the earth, and made it quite reecho with its fall.

II

THREE GREAT ARTISTS OF GREECE[8]

APELLES,[9] of Cos, surpassed all the other painters who either preceded or succeeded him. Single-handed, he contributed more to painting than all the others together, and even went so far as to publish some treatises on the principles of the art. The great point of artistic merit with him was his singular charm of gracefulness, and this too, tho the greatest of painters were his contemporaries. In admiring their works and bestowing high eulogiums upon them, he used to say that there was still wanting in them that ideal of beauty so peculiar to himself, and known to the Greeks as "Charis"; others, he said, had acquired all the other requisites of

[8] From the "Natural History." Translated by John Bostock and H. T. Riley.

[9] Apelles lived in the time of Philip and Alexander the Great. Cos is an island in the Ægean Sea.

perfection, but in this one point he himself had no equal. He also asserted his claim to another great point of merit; admiring a picture by Protogenes, which bore evident marks of unbounded laboriousness and the most minute finish, he remarked that in every respect Protogenes was fully his equal, or perhaps his superior, except in this, that he himself knew when to take his hand off a picture—a memorable lesson, which teaches us that over-carefulness may be productive of bad results. His candor, too, was equal to his talent; he acknowledged the superiority of Melanthius [10] in his grouping, and of Asclepicdorus in the niceness of his measurements, or in other words, the distances that ought to be left between the objects represented.

A circumstance that happened to him in connection with Protogenes [11] is worthy of notice. The latter was living at Rhodes, when Apelles disembarked there, desirous of seeing the works of a man whom he had hitherto only known by reputation. Accordingly, he repaired at once to the studio; Protogenes was not at home, but there happened to be a large panel upon the easel ready for painting, with an old woman who was left in charge. To his inquiries she made answer that Protogenes was not at home; and then asked whom she should name as the visitor. "Here he is," was the reply of Apelles; and seizing a brush, he traced with color upon the

[10] A painter of the Sicyonian school who flourished in the third century B.C.

[11] Protogenes, a native of Caria, in Asia Minor, was celebrated as a painter at Rhodes in the second half of the fourth century B.C.

panel an outline of a singularly minute finer. Upon his return the old woman mentioned Protogenes what had happened. The artist, it is said, upon remarking the delicacy of the touch, instantly exclaimed that Apelles must have been the visitor, for that no other person was capable of executing anything so exquisitely perfect. So saying, he traced within the same outline a still finer outline, but with another color; and then took his departure, with instructions to the woman to show it to the stranger if he returned, and to let him know that this was the person whom he had come to see.

It happened as he anticipated—Apelles returned; and vexed at finding himself thus surpassed, he took up another color and split both of the outlines, leaving no possibility of anything finer being executed. Upon seeing this, Protogenes admitted that he was defeated, and at once flew to the harbor to look for his guest. He thought proper, too, to transmit the panel to posterity, just as it was; and it always continued to be held in the highest admiration by all—artists in particular. I am told that it was burned in the first fire which took place at Cæsar's palace on the Palatine Hill; but in former times I have often stopt to admire it. Upon its vast surface it contained nothing whatever except the three outlines, so remarkably fine as to escape the sight: among the most elaborate works of numerous other artists it had all the appearance of a blank space; and yet by that very fact it attracted the notice of every one, and was held in higher estimation than any other painting there.

It was a custom with Apelles, to which he most tenaciously adhered, never to let any day pass, however busy he might be, without exercising himself by tracing some outline or other; a practise which has now passed into a proverb. It was also a practise with him, when he had completed a work, to exhibit it to the view of the passers-by in some exposed place; while he himself, concealed behind the picture, would listen to the criticisms that were passed upon it: it being his opinion that the judgment of the public was preferable to his own, as being the more discerning of the two. It was under these circumstances, they say, that he was censured by a shoemaker for having represented the shoes with one shoe-string too little. The next day, the shoemaker, quite proud at seeing the former error corrected, thanks to his advice, began to criticize the leg; upon which Apelles, full of indignation, popped his head out, and reminded him that a shoemaker should give no opinion beyond the shoes—a piece of advice which has equally passed into a proverbial saying. In fact, Apelles was a person of great amenity of manners—a circumstance which rendered him particularly agreeable to Alexander the Great, who would often come to his studio. He had forbidden himself by public edict, as already stated, to be represented by any other artist. On one occasion, however, when the prince was in his studio, talking a great deal about painting without knowing anything about it, Apelles quietly begged that he would quit the subject, telling him that he would get laughed at by the boys who were there grinding the colors; so great was the influence which he rightfully possess over a monarch who was otherwise of an irascible temperament. And yet, irascible as he was, Alexander conferred upon him a very signal mark of the high estimation in which he held him: for having, in his admiration of her extraordinary beauty, engaged Apelles to paint Pancaste undraped—the most beloved of all his concubines—the artist while so engaged fell in love with her; upon which, Alexander, perceiving this to be the case, made him a present of her: thus showing himself, tho a great king in courage, a still greater one in self-command—this action redounding no less to his honor than any of his victories.

Superior to all the statues not only of Praxiteles,[12] but of any other artist that ever existed, is his Cnidian Venus; for the inspection of which, many persons before now have purposely undertaken a voyage to Cnidos. The artist made two statues of the goddess, and offered them both for sale: one of them was represented with drapery, and for this reason was preferred by the people of Cos, who had the choice; the second was offered them at the same price, but on the grounds of propriety and modesty they thought fit to choose the other. Upon this, the Cnidians purchased the rejected statue, and immensely superior has it always been held in general estimation. At a later period, King Nicomedes wished to purchase this statue of the Cnidians,

[12] Praxiteles was born in Athens about the end of the fifth century and continued active as an artist until the time of Alexander the Great. Nearly sixty of his works are mentioned in ancient writings, but only two have been identified in modern times.

and made them an offer to pay off the whole of their public debt, which was very large. They preferred, however, to submit to any extremity rather than part with it; and with good reason, for by this statue Praxiteles has perpetuated the glory of Cnidos. The little temple in which it is placed is open on all sides, so that the beauties of the statue admit of being seen from every point of view—an arrangement which was favored by the goddess herself, it is generally believed.

Among all nations which the fame of the Olympian Jupiter has reached, Phidias [18] is looked upon, beyond all doubt, as the most famous of artists; but to let those who have never seen his works know how deservedly he is esteemed, we will take this opportunity of adducing a few slight proofs of the genius which he displayed. In doing this we shall not appeal to the beauty of his Olympian Jupiter, nor yet to the vast proportions of his Athenian Minerva, six-and-twenty cubits in height, and composed of ivory and gold: but it is to the shield of this last statue that we shall draw attention; upon the convex face of which he has chased a combat of the Amazons, while upon the concave side of it he has represented the battle between the gods and the giants. Upon the sandals, again, we see the wars of the Lapithæ and Centaurs; so careful has he been to fill every smallest portion of his work with some proof or other of his artistic skill.

[18] Phidias was born in Athens about 500 B.C. and died about 430.

QUINTILIAN

Born in Spain about 35 A.D.; died about 95; celebrated as rhetorian; educated in Rome, where he taught oratory for twenty years; patronized by the emperors Vespasian and Domitian; his most celebrated work the "Institutio Oratoria."[1]

THE ORATOR MUST BE A GOOD MAN[2]

LET the orator, then, whom I propose to form, be such a one as is characterized by the definition of Marcus Cato, *a good man skilled in speaking*.

But the requisite which Cato has placed first in this definition, that an orator should be *a good man*, is naturally of more estimation and importance than the other. It is of importance that an orator should be good, because, should the power of speaking be a support to evil, nothing would be more pernicious than eloquence alike to public concerns and private, and I myself, who, as far as is in my power, strive to contribute something to the faculty of the orator, should deserve very ill of the world, since I should furnish arms, not for soldiers, but for robbers. May I not draw an argument from the condition of mankind? Nature herself, in

---

[1] Quintilian is notable as a writer who was not influenced by his great contemporary Seneca, whom he disliked and harshly criticized for literary defects. Quintilian modeled his own style on that of Cicero, altho at times he dropt back unconsciously into that of Seneca.

[2] From Book XII, Chapter 1, of the "Institutes of Oratory." Translated by J. S. Watson.

bestowing on man that which she seems to have granted him preeminently, and by which she appears to have distinguished us from all other animals, would have acted, not as a parent, but as a stepmother, if she had designed the faculty of speech to be the promoter of crime, the oppressor of innocence, and the enemy of truth; for it would have been better for us to have been born dumb, and to have been left destitute of reasoning powers, than to have received endowments from providence only to turn them to the destruction of one another.

My judgment carries me still further; for I not only say that he who would answer my idea of an orator must be a good man, but that no man, unless he be good, can ever be an orator. To an orator discernment and prudence are necessary; but we can certainly not allow discernment to those, who when the ways of virtue and vice are set before them, prefer to follow that of vice; nor can we allow them prudence, since they subject themselves, by the unforeseen consequences of their actions, often to the heaviest penalty of the law, and always to that of an evil conscience. But if it be not only truly said by the wise, but always justly believed by the vulgar, that no man is vicious who is not also foolish, a fool, assuredly, will never become an orator.

It is to be further considered that the mind can not be in a condition for pursuing the most noble of studies, unless it be entirely free from vice; not only because there can be no communion of good and evil in the same breast, and to meditate at once on the best things and the worst is no more in the power of the same mind than it is possible for the same man to be at once virtuous and vicious; but also because a mind intent on so arduous a study should be exempt from all other cares, even such as are unconnected with vice; for then, and then only, when it is free and master of itself, and when no other object harasses and distracts its attention, will it be able to keep in view the end to which it is devoted. But if an inordinate attention to an estate, a too anxious pursuit of wealth, indulgence in the pleasures of the chase, and the devotion of our days to public spectacles, rob our studies of much of our time (for whatever time is given to one thing is lost to another), what effect must we suppose that ambition, avarice, and envy will produce, whose excitements are so violent as even to disturb our sleep and our dreams? Nothing indeed is so preoccupied, so unsettled, so torn and lacerated with such numerous and various passions, as a bad mind; for when it intends evil, it is agitated with hope, care, and anxiety, and when it has attained the object of its wickedness, it is tormented with uneasiness, and the dread of every kind of punishment.

No man, certainly, will doubt, that it is the object of all oratory, that what is stated to the judge may appear to him to be true and just; and which of the two, let me ask, will produce such a conviction with the greater ease, the good man or the bad? A good man, doubtless, will speak of what is true and honest with greater frequency; but even if, from being influenced by some call of duty, he endeavors to support what is fallacious (a case which, as I shall show, may sometimes occur), he must still be heard with greater credit than a bad man. But with bad men, on the other hand, dissimulation sometimes fails, as well through their contempt for the opinion of mankind, as through their ignorance of what is right; hence they assert without modesty, and maintain their assertions without shame; and, in attempting what evidently can not be accomplished, there appears in them a repulsive obstinacy and useless perseverance; for bad men, as well in their pleadings as in their lives, entertain dishonest expectations; and it often happens, that even when they speak the truth, belief is not accorded them, and the employment of advocates of such a character is regarded as a proof of the badness of a cause.

I must, however, notice those objections to my opinion, which appear to be clamored forth, as it were, by the general consent of the multitude. Was not then Demosthenes, they ask, a great orator? yet we have heard that he was not a good man. Was not Cicero a great orator? yet many have thrown censure upon his character. To such questions how shall I answer? Great displeasure is likely to be shown at any reply whatever; and the ears of my audience require first to be propitiated. The character of Demosthenes, let me say, does not appear to me deserving of such severe reprehension, that I should believe all the calumnies that are heaped upon him by his enemies, especially when I read his excellent plans for the benefit of his country and the honorable termination of his life. Nor do I see that the feeling of an upright citizen was, in any respect, wanting to Cicero. As proofs of his integrity, may be mentioned his consulship, in which he conducted himself with so much honor, his honorable administration of his province; his refusal to be one of the twenty commissioners; and, during the civil wars, which fell with great severity on his times, his uprightness of mind, which was never swayed, either by hope or by fear, from adhering to the better party, or the supporters of the commonwealth. He is thought by some to have been deficient in courage, but he has given an excellent reply to this charge, when he says that he was timid, not in encountering dangers, but in taking precautions against them; an assertion of which he proved the truth at his death, to which he submitted with the noblest fortitude. But even should the height of virtue have been wanting to these eminent men, I shall reply to those who ask me whether they were orators as the Stoics reply when they are asked whether Zeno, Cleanthes, and Chrysippus were wise men; they say that they were great and deserving of veneration, but that they did not attain the highest excellence of which human nature is susceptible.

Pythagoras desired to be called, not wise, like those who preceded him, but a lover of wisdom. I, however, in speaking of Cicero, have often said, according to the common mode of speech, and shall continue to say, that he was a perfect orator, as we term our friends, in ordinary discourse, good and prudent men, tho such epithets can be justly given only to the perfectly wise. But when I have to speak precisely, and in conformity with the exactness of truth, I shall express myself as longing to see such an orator as he himself also longed to see; for tho I acknowledge that Cicero stood at the head of eloquence, and that I can scarcely find a passage in his speeches to which anything can be added, however many I might find which I may imagine that he would have pruned (for the learned have in general been of opinion that he had numerous excellencies and some faults, and he himself says that he had cut off most of his juvenile exuberance), yet, since he did not claim to himself, tho he had no mean opinion of his merits, the praise of perfection, and since he might certainly have spoken better if a longer life had been granted him, and a more tranquil season for composition, I may not unreasonably believe that the summit of excellence was not attained by him, to which, notwithstanding, no man made nearer approaches. If I had thought otherwise, I might have maintained my opinion with still greater determination and freedom. Did Marcus Antonius declare that he had seen no man truly eloquent, tho to be eloquent is much less than to be a perfect orator; does Cicero himself say that he is still seeking for an orator, and merely conceives and imagines one; and shall I fear to say that in that portion of eternity which is yet to come something may arise still more excellent than what has yet been seen? I take no advantage of the opinion of those who refuse to allow great merit to Cicero and Demosthenes even in eloquence; tho Demosthenes, indeed, does not appear sufficiently near perfection even to Cicero himself, who says that he sometimes nods; nor does Cicero appear so to Brutus and Calvus, who certainly find fault with his language.

TACITUS

Born about 55 A.D.; died about 117; celebrated as historian and orator; prætor in 88; Consul in 97; a friend of the younger Pliny; son-in-law of Agricola; his extant works include a dialog of oratory, a biography of Agricola, "Germania," a history of Rome from Galba to Domitian, and his "Annals," which are a history of the Julian dynasty.[1]

I

FROM REPUBLICAN TO IMPERIAL ROME[2]

KINGS held dominion in the city of Rome from its foundation: Lucius Brutus instituted liberty and the consulate. Dictatorships were resorted to in temporary emergencies: neither the power of the decemvirs continued in force beyond two years, nor the consular authority of the military tribunes for any length of time. The domination of Cinna did not continue long, nor that of Sulla: the influence of Pompey and Crassus quickly merged in Cæsar: the arms of Lepidus and Antony in Augustus, who, with the title of

[1] "If by eloquence is meant the ability to persuade, then Tacitus," according to Cruttwell, "is the most eloquent historian that ever existed." His portraits, especially those of Tiberius and Nero, have been severely criticized by French and English writers, but while his verdicts have been shaken, they have not been reversed. The world still fails to doubt their substantial reality. Tacitus, adds Cruttwell, has probably exercised upon readers a greater power than any other writer of prose whom Rome produced.

[2] From Book I of the "Annals." The Oxford translation revised.

prince, took under his command the commonwealth, exhausted with civil dissensions. But the affairs of the ancient Roman people, whether prosperous or adverse, have been recorded by writers of renown. Nor were there wanting authors of distinguished genius to have composed the history of the times of Augustus, till by the spirit of flattery, which became prevalent, they were deterred. As to Tiberius, Caligula, Claudius, and Nero, whilst they yet reigned the histories of their times were falsified through fear; and after they had fallen, they were written under the influence of recent detestation. Thence my own design of recounting a few incidents respecting Augustus, and those toward the latter part of his life; and, after that, of giving a history of the reign of Tiberius and the rest; uninfluenced by resentment and partiality, as I stand aloof from the causes of them.

When, after the fall of Brutus and Cassius, there remained none to fight for the commonwealth; when Sextus Pompeius was utterly defeated at Sicily; and Lepidus being deprived of his command, and Mark Antony slain, there remained no leader even to the Julian party but Octavius; having put off the name of triumvir, styling himself Consul, and pretending that all he aimed at was the jurisdiction attached to the tribuneship for the protection of the commons; when he had cajoled the soldiery by donations, the people by distribution of corn, and men in general by the charms of peace, he (Octavius) began by gradations to exalt himself over them; to draw to himself the functions of the senate and of the magistrate, and the framing of the laws; in which he was thwarted by no man: the boldest spirits having fallen in some or other of the regular battles, or by proscription; and the surviving nobility being distinguished by wealth and public honors, according to the measure of their promptness to bondage; and as these innovations had been the cause of aggrandizement to them, preferring the present state of things with safety to the revival of ancient liberty with personal peril. Neither were the provinces averse to that condition of affairs; since they mistrusted the government of the senate and people, on account of the contentions among the great and the avarice of the magistrates: while the protection of the laws was enfeebled and borne down by violence, intrigue, and bribery.

Moreover, Augustus, as supports to his domination, raised his sister's son, Claudius Marcellus,[3] a mere youth, to the dignity of pontiff and curule ædile; aggrandized by two successive consulships Marcus Agrippa,[4] a man meanly born, but an accomplished soldier, and the companion of his victories; and soon, on the death of Marcellus, chose him for his son-in-law. The sons of his wife, Tiberius Nero and Claudius Drusus, he dignified with the title of Imperator, tho there had been no diminution in the members of his

[3] Marcellus was the son of Octavia by her husband C. Claudius Marcellus. He married Julia, a daughter of Augustus.

[4] Agrippa was the leading administrative mind under Augustus, with whom he had served in the Civil War and in the battle Actium. The Pantheon, the only complete building of Imperial Rome that still survives, was finished and dedicated by him. He married as his third wife Julia, the widow of Marcellus.

house. For into the family of the Cæsars he had already adopted Lucius and Caius, the sons of Agrippa; and tho they had not yet laid aside the puerile garment, vehement had been his ambition to see them declared princes of the Roman youth, and even designed to the consulship; while he affected to decline the honors for them. Upon the decease of Agrippa, they were cut off, either by a death premature but natural, or by the arts of their stepmother Livia; Lucius on his journey to the armies in Spain, Caius on his return from Armenia, ill of a wound: and as Drusus had been long since dead, Tiberius Nero was the only survivor of his stepsons. On him every honor was accumulated (to that quarter all things inclined); he was by Augustus adopted for his son, assumed colleague in the empire, partner in the tribunitian authority, and presented to the several armies; not from the secret machinations of his mother, as heretofore, but at her open suit. For over Augustus, now very aged, she had obtained such absolute sway, that he banished into the isle of Planasia his only surviving grandson, Agrippa Posthumus; a person destitute indeed of liberal accomplishments, and a man of clownish brutality with great bodily strength, but convicted of no heinous offense. The emperor, strange to say, set Germanicus, the son of Drusus, over eight legions quartered upon the Rhine, and ordered that he should be engrafted into his family by Tiberius by adoption, tho Tiberius had then a son of his own on the verge of manhood; but the object was that he might stand firm by having many to support and protect him. War at that time there remained none,

TACITUS

except that in Germany, kept on foot rather to blot out the disgrace sustained by the loss of Quintilius Varus, with his army, than from any ambition to enlarge the empire, or for any advantage worth contending for. In profound tranquillity were affairs at Rome. The magistrates retained their wonted names; of the Romans, the younger sort had been born since the battle of Actium, and even most of the old during the civil wars: how few were then living who had seen the ancient free state!

The character of the government thus totally changed; no traces were to be found of the spirit of ancient institutions. The system by which every citizen shared in the government being thrown aside, all men regarded the orders of the prince as the only rule of conduct and obedience; nor felt they any anxiety for the present, while Augustus, yet in the vigor of life, maintained the credit of himself and house, and the peace of the state. But when old age had crept over him, and he was sinking under bodily infirmities—when his end was at hand, and thence a new source of hopes and views was presented —some few there were who began to talk idly about the blessings of liberty: many dreaded a civil war—others longed for one; while far the greatest part were occupied in circulating various surmises reflecting upon those who seemed likely to be their masters: "That Agrippa was naturally stern and savage, and exasperated by contumely; and neither in age nor experience equal to a task of such magnitude. Tiberius, indeed, had arrived at fulness of years, and was a distinguished captain, but possest the inveterate and inherent pride of the Claudian family; and many indications of cruel nature escaped him, in spite of all his arts to disguise it; that even from his early infancy he had been trained up in an imperial house; that consulships and triumphs had been accumulated upon him while but a youth. Not even during the years of his abode at Rhodes, where under the plausible name of retirement, he was in fact an exile, did he employ himself otherwise than in meditating future vengeance, studying the arts of simulation, and practising secret and abominable sensualities. That to these considerations was added that of his mother, a woman with the ungovernable spirit peculiar to her sex; that the Romans must be under bondage to a woman, and moreover to two youths, who would meanwhile oppress the state, and, at one time or other, rend it piecemeal."

While the public mind was agitated by these and similar discussions, the illness of Augustus grew daily more serious, and some suspected nefarious practises on the part of his wife. For some months before, a rumor had gone abroad that Augustus, having singled out a few to whom he communicated his purpose, had taken Fabius Maximus for his only companion, had sailed over to the island of Planasia, to visit Agrippa; that many tears were shed on both sides, many tokens of mutual tenderness shown, and hopes from thence conceived that the youth would be restored to the household gods of his grandfather. That Maximus had disclosed this to Martia, his wife—she to Livia; and that the emperor was informed of it: and that Maximus, not long after, dying (it is doubtful whether naturally or by means sought for the purpose), Martia was observed, in her lamentations at his funeral, to upbraid herself as the cause of her husband's destruction. Howsoever that matter might have been, Tiberius was scarce entered Illyrium when he was summoned by a letter from his mother, forwarded with speed, nor is it fully known whether, at his return to Nola,[s] he found Augustus yet breathing, or already lifeless. For Livia had carefully beset the palace, and all the avenues to it, with vigilant guards; and favorable bulletins were from time to time given out, until, the provisions which the conjuncture required being completed, in one and the same moment were published the departure of Augustus, and the accession of Tiberius.

II

THE FUNERAL OF GERMANICUS[e]
(19 A.D.)

AGRIPPINA,[f] continuing her course without the least intermission through all the perils and rigors of a sea-voyage in the winter, arrived at

[s] Nola lay sixteen miles northeast of Naples. The reference is to Drusus, son of Tiberius, and to Germanicus, at that time commanding on the Rhine.

[e] From Book III of the "Annals." The Oxford translation revised.

[f] This Agrippina was the daughter of Agrippa and Julia. She married Germanicus, became the mother of Caligula, and was a woman of lofty character, who died by voluntary starvation after having been exiled by Tiberius.

the island Corcyra, situated over against the shores of Calabria. Unable to moderate her grief, and impatient from inexperience of affliction, she spent a few days there to tranquillize her troubled spirit; when, on hearing of her arrival, all the intimate friends of her family, and most of the officers who had served under Germanicus, with a number of strangers from the neighboring municipal towns, some thinking it due as a mark of respect to the prince, but the greater part carried along with the current, rushed to the city of Brundusium, the readiest port in her way, and the safest landing. As soon as the fleet appeared in the deep, instantly were filled, not the port alone and adjacent parts of the sea, but the walls and roofs, and wherever the most distant prospect could be obtained, with a sorrowing multitude, earnestly asking each other "whether they should receive her on landing in silence, or with some expression of feeling?" Nor was it clearly determined what course would be most suitable to the occasion, when the fleet came slowly in, not as usual in sprightly trim, but all wearing the impress of sadness. When she descended from the ship, accompanied by her two infants,[3] and bearing in her hand the funeral urn, her eyes fixt stedfastly upon the earth, one simultaneous groan burst from the whole assemblage; nor could you distinguish relations from strangers, nor the wailings of men from those of women; nor could any difference be discerned, except that those

[3] It has been conjectured that the two children of Germanicus here referred to were Caligula, who had gone to the East with his father, and Julia, who was born in Lesbos.

who came to meet her, in the vehemence of recent grief, surpassed the attendants of Agrippina, who were exhausted with continued mourning.

Tiberius had dispatched two prætorian cohorts, with directions that the magistrates of Calabria, with Apulians and Campanians, should pay their last offices of respect to the memory of his son; upon the shoulders, therefore, of the tribunes and centurions his ashes were borne; before them were carried the ensigns unadorned, and the fasces reversed. As they passed through the colonies, the populace in black, the knights in their purple robes, burned precious raiment, perfumes, and whatever else is used in funeral solemnities, according to the ability of the place; even they whose cities lay remote from the route, came forth, offered victims, and erected altars to the gods of the departed, and with tears and ejaculations testified their sorrow. Drusus came as far as Terracina, with Claudius the brother of Germanicus, and those of his children who had been left at Rome.[9] The Consuls, Marcus Valerius and Marcus Aurelius[10] (for they had now entered upon their office), the senate, and great part of the people, filled the road—a scattered procession, each walking and expressing his grief as inclination led him; in sooth, flattery was an utter stranger here, for all knew how real was the joy, how hollow the grief, of Tiberius for the death of Germanicus.

[9] These children were Nero, Drusus, Agrippina and Drusilla.

[10] Not the Emperor of that name, who was not born until 121 A.D.

Tiberius and Livia [11] avoided appearing abroad —public lamentation they thought below their dignity—or perhaps they apprehended that if their countenances were examined by all eyes their hypocrisy would be detected. That Antonia, mother to the deceased, bore any part in the funeral, I do not find either in the historians or in the journals, tho, besides Agrippina, and Drusus, and Claudius, his other relations are likewise there recorded by name; whether by sickness she was prevented, or whether her soul, vanquished by sorrow, could not bear to go through the representation of such an overpowering calamity. I would rather believe her constrained by Tiberius and Livia, who left not the palace, that they might seem to grieve alike, and that the grandmother and uncle might appear to have followed her example in staying at home.

The day on which his remains were deposited in the tomb of Augustus, at one time exhibited the silence of perfect desolation; at another, the uproar of vociferous lamentation; the streets of the city were crowded, one general blaze of torches glared throughout the Campus Martius; there the soldiers under arms, the magistrates without the insignia of office, and the people ranged according to their tribes, passionately exclaimed, "that the commonwealth was utterly lost, that henceforth there remained no hope," so openly and so boldly that you would have believed they had forgotten those who ruled over them. But nothing pierced Tiberius more deeply

[11] Mother of Tiberius by a husband whom she had married before she married Augustus.

than the warm interest excited in favor of Agrippina, while they gave her such titles as "the ornament of her country, the only blood of Augustus, an unparalleled example of primitive virtue"; and, looking up to heaven and the gods, they implored "the preservation of her issue, and that they might outlive their oppressors."

There were those who missed the pomp of a public funeral, and compared with this the superior honors and magnificence displayed by Augustus in that of Drusus, the father of Germanicus; observing, "that he himself had traveled, in the depth of winter, as far as Ticinus, and, continuing by the corpse, had with it entered the city; around his bier were crowded the images of the Claudii and Julii; he was mourned in the forum; his encomium pronounced on the rostra; all the honors invented by our ancestors, or added by their posterity, were heaped upon him. But to Germanicus were denied the ordinary solemnities, and such as were due to every distinguished Roman. Certainly his corpse was burned in a foreign country because of the long journey, in such a manner as it was, but afterward it was but just to have compensated the scantiness of the first ceremony by the increased solemnity of the last; his brother met him but one day's journey, his uncle not even at the gate. Where were those observances of the ancients, the effigies of the dead laid in state on a bed, hymns composed in memory of departed virtue, with encomiums and tears? Where at least the ceremonial of sorrow?"

All this was known to Tiberius, and to suppress the reflections of the populace, he admonished them in an edict, "that many illustrious Romans had died for the commonwealth, but none so universally and vehemently regretted; and that it was to the honor of himself and all others, if bounds were observed. The same things which became private families and small states, became not princes and an imperial people; that it was not unseemly to lament in the first transport of sorrow, nay, relief was afforded by weeping, but it was now time to recover and compose their minds. Thus the deified Julius, upon the loss of an only daughter;[12] thus the deified Augustus, upon the premature death of his grandsons, had both concealed their sorrow. More ancient examples were unnecessary; how often had the Roman people sustained with equanimity the slaughter of their armies, the death of their generals, and entire destruction of illustrious families—princes were mortal, the commonwealth was eternal—they should therefore resume their customary vocations." And because the spectacle of the Megalesian games was at hand, he added, "that they should even lay aside their grief for amusements."

The vacation ended, public affairs were resumed; Drusus departed for the army in Illyricum, the minds of all men impatiently looking for vengeance upon Piso; and amidst many complaints, that while he was roaming at large through the delightful regions of Asia and Greece, he was undermining by contemptuous and artful delay the evidences of his crimes; for it was generally known that Martina, that

[12] Julia, daughter of Julius Cæsar by his wife Cornelia.

notorious trafficker in sorceries, and sent, as I have above related, by Cneius Sentius to Rome, had died suddenly at Brundusium; that poison lay concealed in a knot of her hair.

III

THE DEATH OF SENECA [13]
(65 A.D.)

The next death added by Nero was that of Plautius Lateranus, consul elect; and with such precipitation, that he would not allow him to embrace his children, nor the usual brief interval to choose his mode of death. He was dragged to the place allotted for the execution of slaves, and there, by the hand of Statius the tribune, slaughtered. In his death he maintained the most invincible silence, not charging his executioner with participation in the design for which he suffered. The destruction of Seneca followed, to the infinite joy of the prince; not because he had ascertained that he was a party to the conspiracy, but that he might assail him with the sword, since poison had failed: for Natalis only had named him; and his disclosure amounted but to this, "that he had been sent by Piso [14] to visit

[13] From Book XV of the "Annals." The Oxford translation revised.

[14] Caius Piso, leader of an unsuccessful conspiracy against Nero in 65. Other famous Romans of the name of Piso are Lucius, censor, consul and author; another Lucius whose daughter was married to Julius Cæsar; and Cneius, governor of Syria, who was accused of murdering Germanicus.

Seneca, then indisposed, to complain that he was refused admittance; and to represent, that it would be better if they maintained their friendship by intercourse: that to this Seneca replied, that talking to each other and frequent interviews were to the service of neither; but upon the safety of Piso his own security rested." Granius Silvanus, tribune of a pretorian cohort, was ordered to represent this to Seneca, and to demand of him, "whether he admitted the words of Natalis, and his own answers." Seneca had that very day, either from chance or design, returned from Campania, and rested at a villa of his, four miles from Rome: thither arrived the tribune toward evening, and beset the villa with his men; and then, as he sat at table with Paulline his wife, and two friends, delivered his orders from the emperor.

Seneca replied, "that Natalis had in truth been sent to him, and in the name of Piso complained, that he was debarred from visiting him; and that he had excused himself on the score of illness and his love of retirement; but he had no motive to declare that he preferred the safety of a private man to his own security; nor was his disposition prone to flattery; as no man better knew than Nero, who had experienced more frequent proofs of the freedom than the servility of Seneca."

When this answer was by the tribune reported to Nero, in presence of Poppæa [15] and Tigellinus,

[15] Poppæa Sabina, who once was the wife of Otho and mistress of Nero. She was afterward divorced from Otho and married to Nero in 62 A.D. She died from the effects of a kick given by Nero.

TACITUS

who composed the cabinet council, the raging tyrant asked, whether Seneca meditated a voluntary death? the tribune averred "that he had manifested no symptoms of fear; and neither in his words nor looks did he detect any indication of regret." He was therefore commanded to return, and tell him he was doomed to die. Fabius Rusticus writes, "that the tribune did not return by the road he went, but turning off went to Fenius, captain of the guards, and stating to him the emperor's orders, asked whether he should obey him; and was by him admonished to execute them"; thus displaying that want of spirit which by some fatality prevailed universally; for Silvanus too was one of the conspirators, and yet was contributing to multiply the atrocities he had conspired to avenge. He avoided, however, seeing and speaking to Seneca; but sent in a centurion to apprize him of his final doom.

Seneca undismayed, called for tables to make his will; and, as this was prohibited by the centurion, turning to his friends, he told them, "that since he was debarred from requiting their services, he bequeathed them that which alone was now left him, but which yet was the fairest legacy he had to leave them—the example of his life: and if they kept it in view, they would reap the fame due to honorable acquirements and inviolable friendship." At the same time he endeavored to repress their tears and restore their fortitude, now by soothing language, and now in a more animated strain and in a tone of rebuke, asking them, "where were the precepts of philosophy? where the rules of conduct under impending evils, studied for so many years? For who was unapprized of the ferocious disposition of Nero? Nor could anything else be expected after he had murdered his mother and brother, than that he should proceed to destroy his nursing father and preceptor."

After these and similar reasonings addrest to the company in general, he embraced his wife; and after a brief but vigorous effort to get the better of the apprehensions that prest upon him at that moment, he besought and implored her "to refrain from surrendering herself to endless grief; but endeavor to mitigate her regret for her husband by means of those honorable consolations which she would experience in the contemplation of his virtuous life." Paulina, on the contrary, urged her purpose to die with him, and called for the hand of the executioner. When Seneca, unwilling to impede her glory, and also from affection, as he was anxious not to leave one who was dear to him above everything, exposed to the hard usage of the world, thus addrest her: "I had pointed out to you how to soften the ills of life; but you prefer the renown of dying: I will not envy you the honor of the example. Tho both display the same unflinching fortitude in encountering death; still the glory of your exit will be superior to mine." After this, both had the veins of their arms opened with the same stroke. As the blood flowed slowly from the aged body of Seneca, attenuated as it was too by scanty sustenance, he had the veins of his legs and hams also cut; and unable to bear up under the excessive torture, lest by his own sufferings he should overpower the resolution of his wife, and by witnessing her anguish be betrayed into impatience himself, he advised her to retire into another chamber. His eloquence continued to flow during the latest moments of his existence, and summoning his secretaries, he dictated many things, which, as they have been published in his own words, I forbear to exhibit in other language.

IV

THE BURNING OF ROME BY ORDER OF NERO[16]
(64 A.D.)

THERE followed a dreadful disaster; whether fortuitously, or by the wicked contrivance of the prince,[17] is not determined, for both are asserted by historians: but of all the calamities which ever befell this city from the rage of fire, this was the most terrible and severe. It broke out in that part of the Circus which is contiguous to mounts Palatine and Cœlius; where, by reason of shops in which were kept such goods as minister aliment to fire, the moment it commenced it acquired strength, and being accelerated by the wind, it spread at once through the whole extent of the Circus: for neither were the houses

[16] From Book XV of the "Annals." The Oxford translation revised.

[17] Nero.

secured by enclosures, nor the temples environed with walls, nor was there any other obstacle to intercept its progress; but the flame, spreading every way impetuously, invaded first the lower regions of the city, then mounted to the higher; then again ravaging the lower, it baffled every effort to extinguish it, by the rapidity of its destructive course, and from the liability of the city to conflagration, in consequence of the narrow and intricate alleys, and the irregularity of the streets in ancient Rome.[18] Add to this, the wailings of terrified women, the infirm condition of the aged, and the helplessness of childhood: such as strove to provide for themselves, and those who labored to assist others; these dragging the feeble, those waiting for them; some hurrying, others lingering; altogether created a scene of universal confusion and embarrassment: and while they looked back upon the danger in their rear, they often found themselves beset before, and on their sides: or if they had escaped into the quarters adjoining, these too were already seized by the devouring flames; even the parts which they believed remote and exempt, were found to be in the same distress. At last, not knowing what to shun, or where to seek sanctu-

---

[18] Suetonius relates that, when some one repeated to Nero the line "When I am dead, let fire devour the world," he replied, "Let it be whilst I am living." That author asserts that Nero's purpose sprung in part from his dislike of old buildings and narrow streets. During the progress of the fire several men of consular rank met Nero's domestic servants with torches and combustibles which they were using to start fires, but did not dare to stay their hands. Livy asserts that, after it was destroyed by the Gauls, Rome had been rebuilt with narrow winding streets.

ary, they crowded the streets, and lay along in the open fields. Some, from the loss of their whole substance, even the means of their daily sustenance, others, from affection for their relations, whom they had not been able to snatch from the flames, suffered themselves to perish in them, tho they had opportunity to escape. Neither dared any man offer to check the fire: so repeated were the menaces of many who forbade to extinguish it; and because others openly threw firebrands, with loud declarations "that they had one who authorized them"; whether they did it that they might plunder with the less restraint, or in consequence of orders given.

Nero, who was at that juncture sojourning at Antium,[19] did not return to the city till the fire approached that quarter of his house which connected the palace with the gardens of Mæcenas;[20] nor could it, however, be prevented from devouring the house and palace, and everything around. But for the relief of the people, thus destitute, and driven from their dwellings, he opened the fields of Mars and the monumental edifices erected by Agrippa,[21] and even his own gardens. He likewise reared temporary houses for the reception of the forlorn multitude: and from Ostia and the neighboring cities were brought, up the river, household necessaries; and the price of grain was reduced to three sesterces the measure. All which proceedings, tho of a

[19] A city in the central Apennines, six miles from Lake Fucinus.

[20] Near the Esquiline.

[21] The house, gardens, baths and the Pantheon of Agrippa are here referred to. Nero's gardens were near the Vatican.

popular character, were thrown away, because a rumor had become universally current, "that the very time when the city was in flames, Nero, going on the stage of his private theater, sang 'The Destruction of Troy,' assimilating the present disaster to that catastrophe of ancient times."

At length, on the sixth day, the conflagration was stayed at the foot of Esquilliæ, by pulling down an immense quantity of buildings, so that an open space, and, as it were, void air, might check the raging element by breaking the continuity. But ere the consternation had subsided, the fire broke out afresh, with no little violence, but in regions more spacious, and therefore with less destruction of human life: but more extensive havoc was made of the temples, and the porticoes dedicated to amusement. This conflagration, too was the subject of more censorious remark, as it arose in the Æmilian possessions of Tigellinus: and Nero seemed to aim at the glory of building a new city, and calling it by his own name: for, of the fourteen sections into which Rome is divided, four were still standing entire, three were leveled with the ground, and in the seven others there remained only here and there a few remnants of houses, shattered and half-consumed.

It were no easy task to recount the number of tenements and temples which were lost: but the following, most venerable for antiquity and sanctity, were consumed: that dedicated by Servius Tullius to the Moon; the temple and great altar consecrated by Evander the Arcadian to Hercules while present; the chapel vowed by

Romulus to Jupiter Stator; the palace of Numa,[22] with the temple of Vesta, and in it the tutelar gods of Rome. Moreover, the treasures accumulated by so many victories, the beautiful productions of Greek artists, ancient writings of authors celebrated for genius, and till then preserved entire, were consumed: and tho great was the beauty of the city, in its renovated form, the older inhabitants remembered many decorations of the ancient which could not be replaced in the modern city. There were some who remarked that the commencement of this fire showed itself on the fourteenth before the calends of July, the day on which the Senones set fire to the captured city. Others carried their investigation so far as to determine that an equal number of years, months, and days intervened between the two fires.

To proceed: Nero appropriated to his own purposes the ruins of his country, and founded upon them a palace; in which the old-fashioned, and, in those luxurious times, common ornaments of gold and precious stones, were not so much the objects of attraction as lands and lakes; in one part, woods like vast deserts; in another part, open spaces and expansive prospects. The projectors and superintendents of this plan were Severus and Celer, men of such ingenuity and daring enterprise as to attempt to conquer by art the obstacles of nature, and fool away the treasures of the prince: they had even undertaken to sink a navigable canal from the lake Avernus to the mouth of the Tiber, over an arid shore, or through opposing mountains: nor indeed does

[22] The palace of Numa, on the Palatine hill, had been the mansion of Augustus.

there occur anything of a humid nature for supplying water, except the Pomptine marshes; the rest is either craggy rock or a parched soil: and had it even been possible to break through these obstructions, the toil had been intolerable, and disproportioned to the object. Nero, however, who longed to achieve things that exceeded credibility, exerted all his might to perforate the mountains adjoining to Avernus: and to this day there remain traces of his abortive project.

But the rest of the old site not occupied by his palace, was laid out, not as after the Gallic fire, without discrimination and regularity, but with the lines of streets measured out, broad spaces left for transit, the height of the buildings limited, open areas left, and porticoes added to protect the front of the clustered dwellings: these porticoes Nero engaged to rear at his own expense, and then to deliver to each proprietor the areas about them cleared. He moreover proposed rewards proportioned to every man's rank and private substance, and fixt a day within which, if their houses, single or clustered, were finished, they should receive them: he appointed the marshes of Ostia for a receptacle of the rubbish, and that the vessels which had conveyed grain up the Tiber should return laden with rubbish; that the buildings themselves should be raised to a certain portion of their height without beams, and arched with stone from the quarries of Gabii or Alba, that stone being proof against fire: that over the water springs, which had been improperly intercepted by private individuals, overseers should be placed, to provide for their flowing in greater abundance, and in a greater number of places, for the supply of the public: that every housekeeper should have in his yard means for extinguishing fire; neither should there be party-walls, but every house should be enclosed by its own walls. These regulations, which were favorably received, in consideration of their utility, were also a source of beauty to the new city: yet some there were who believed that the ancient form was more conducive to health, as from the narrowness of the streets and the height of the buildings the rays of the sun were more excluded; whereas now, the spacious breadth of the streets, without any shade to protect it, was more intensely heated in warm weather.

Such were the provisions made by human counsels. The gods were next addrest with expiations; and recourse had to the Sibyl's books. By admonition from them to Vulcan, Ceres, and Proserpina, supplicatory sacrifices were made, and Juno propitiated by the matrons, first in the Capitol, then upon the nearest shore, where, by water drawn from the sea, the temple and image of the goddess were besprinkled; and the ceremony of placing the goddess in her sacred chair, and her vigil, were celebrated by ladies who had husbands. But not all the relief that could come from man, not all the bounties that the prince could bestow, nor all the atonements which could be presented to the gods, availed to relieve Nero from the infamy of being believed to have ordered the conflagration.

Hence, to suppress the rumor, he falsely charged with the guilt, and punished with the most exquisite tortures, the persons commonly called Christians,[23] who were hated for their enormities. Christus, the founder of that name, was put to death as a criminal by Pontius Pilate, procurator of Judea, in the reign of Tiberius: but the pernicious superstition, represt for a time, broke out again, not only through Judea, where the mischief originated, but through the city of Rome also, whither all things horrible and disgraceful flow, from all quarters, as to a common receptacle, and where they are encouraged. Accordingly, first those were seized who confest they were Christians; next, on their information, a vast multitude were convicted, not so much on the charge of burning the city, as of hating the human race. And in their deaths they were also made the subjects of sport, for they were covered with the hides of wild beasts, and worried to death by dogs, or nailed to crosses, or set fire to, and when day declined, burned to serve for nocturnal lights. Nero offered his own gardens for that spectacle, and exhibited a Circensian game, indiscriminately mingling with the common people in the habit of a charioteer, or else standing in his chariot. Whence a feeling of compassion arose toward the sufferers, tho guilty and deserving to be made examples of by capital punishment, because they seemed not to be cut off for the public good, but victims to the ferocity of one man.[24]

[23] Carlyle, in his essay on Voltaire, refers to this passage as having been "inserted as a small, transitory, altogether trifling circumstance, in the history of such a potentate as Nero"; but it has become "to us the most earnest, sad and sternly significant passage that we know to exist in writing."

[24] Claudius already had expelled the Jews from Rome and included in their number the followers of Christ. But his

TACITUS

In the meantime, in order to supply money, all Italy was pillaged, the provinces ruined: both the people in alliance with us, and the states which are called free. Even the gods were not exempt from plunder on this occasion, their temples in the city being despoiled, and all the gold conveyed away, which the Roman people, in every age, either in gratitude for triumphs, or in fulfilment of vows, had consecrated, in times of prosperity, or in seasons of dismay. Through Greece and Asia, indeed, the gifts and oblations, and even the statues of the deities, were carried off; Acratus and Secundus Carinas being sent into those provinces for the purpose: the former, Nero's freedman, a prompt instrument in any iniquity; the other, acquainted with Greek learning, as far as relates to lip-knowledge, but unadorned with virtuous accomplishments. Of Seneca it was reported, "that to avert from himself the odium of this sacrilege, he prayed to retire to a seat of his, remote from Rome, and being refused, feigned indisposition, as tho his nerves were affected, and confined himself to his chamber." Some authors have recorded, "that a freedman of his, named Cleonicus, had, by the command of Nero, prepared poison for his master, who escaped it, either from the discovery made by the freedman, or from the caution inspired by his own apprehensions, as he supported nature by a diet perfectly simple, satisfying the cravings of hunger by wild fruits, and the solicitations of thirst from the running brook."

edict was not specifically directed against the Christians. Nero was the first emperor who persecuted them as professors of a new faith.

THE BEST OF THE WORLD'S CLASSICS

V

THE BURNING OF THE CAPITOL AT ROME[25]
(69 A.D.)

MARTIALIS had scarcely reentered the Capitol, when the furious soldiers appeared before it, without a general, and each man acting on his own suggestions. Having rapidly passed the forum, and the temples that overlook it, they marched up the opposite hill, as far as the first gates of the citadel. On the right side of the ascent, a range of porticoes had been built in ancient times. Going out upon the roof of those, the besieged threw a shower of stones and tiles. The assailants had no weapons but their swords, and to fetch engines and missiles seemed a tedious delay. They threw brands into the portico that jutted near them. They followed up the fire, and would have forced their way through the gate of the Capitol, which the fire had laid hold of, if Sabinus had not placed as a barrier in the very approach, in lieu of a wall, the statues, those honorable monuments of our ancestors, which were pulled down wherever they could be found. They then assaulted the Capitol in two different quarters; near the grove of the asylum, and where the Tarpeian rock is ascended by a hundred steps. Both attacks were unfore-

---

[25] From Book III of the "History." The Oxford translation revised. Pliny, Josephus and Dio all agree that the Capitol was set on fire by the followers of Vitellius.

seen. That by the asylum was the nearer and most vigorous. Nor could they be stopt from climbing up the contiguous buildings, which being raised high under the idea of undisturbed peace, reach the basement of the Capitol. Here a doubt exists whether the fire was thrown upon the roofs by the storming party or the besieged, the latter being more generally supposed to have done it, to repulse those who were climbing up, and had advanced some way. The fire extended itself thence to the porticoes adjoining the temples; soon the eagles that supported the cupola caught fire, and as the timber was old they fed the flame. Thus the Capitol, with its gates shut, neither stormed, nor defended, was burned to the ground.

From the foundation of the city to that hour, the Roman republic had felt no calamity so deplorable, so shocking, as that, unassailed by a foreign enemy, and, were it not for the vices of the age, with the deities propitious, the temple of Jupiter supremely good and great, built by our ancestors with solemn auspices, the pledge of empire, which neither Porsena,[26] when Rome surrendered to his arms, nor the Gauls,[27] when they captured the city, were permitted to violate, should be now demolished by the madness of the rulers of the state. The Capitol was once before destroyed by fire during a civil war; but

[26] Porsena did not actually get into Rome, being induced to raise the siege when only at its gates.

[27] The capture of Rome by the Gauls under Brennus took place in 390 B.C. The destruction of the Capitol in the first Civil War occurred in 83 B.C., during the consulship of Lucius Scipio and Caius Norbaius. The fire was not started as an act of open violence, however, but by clandestine incendiaries.

it was from the guilty machinations of private individuals. Now it was besieged publicly, publicly set fire to; and what were the motives for the war? what was the object to be gained, that so severe a calamity was incurred? Warred we in our country's cause?—Tarquinius Priscus, during the war with the Sabines, built it in fulfilment of a vow, and laid the foundations more in conformity with his anticipations of the future grandeur of the empire, than the limited extent of the Roman means at that time. Servius Tullius, assisted by the zeal of the allies of Rome, and after him Tarquin the Proud, with the spoils of Suessa Pometia, added to the building. But the glory of completing the design was reserved for the era of liberty. When tyrants were swept away, Horatius Pulvilus, in his second consulship, dedicated the temple, finished with such magnificence that the wealth of after ages graced it with new embellishments, but added nothing to its dimensions. Four hundred and fifteen years afterward, in the consulship of Lucius Scipio and Caius Norbanus, it was burned to the ground, and again rebuilt on the old foundation. Sulla having now triumphed over his opponents, undertook to build it, but nevertheless did not dedicate it; the only thing wanting to crown his felicity. That honor was reserved for Lutatius Catulus, whose name, amidst so many works of the Cæsars, remained legible till the days of Vitellius. Such was the sacred building which was at this time reduced to ashes.

TACITUS

VI

THE SIEGE OF CREMONA [28]
(69 A.D.)

WHEN they came to Cremona, they found a new and enormous difficulty. In the war with Otho, the German legions had formed a camp round the walls of the town, and fortified it with lines of circumvallation. New works were added afterward. The victors stood astonished at the sight, and even the generals were at a stand, undecided what orders to give. With troops harassed by exertions through the night and day, to carry the place by storm was difficult, and, without succors at hand, might be dangerous; but if they marched to Bedriacum, the fatigue would be insupportable, and the victory would end in nothing. To throw up intrenchments was dangerous, in the face of an enemy, who might suddenly sally forth and put them to the rout, while employed on the work in detached parties. A difficulty still greater than all arose from the temper of the men, more patient of danger than delay: inasmuch as a state of security afforded no excitement, while hope grew out of enterprise, however perilous; and carnage, wounds and

---

[28] From Book III of the "History." The Oxford translation revised. Near Cremona had been fought the first battle of Bedriacum by the armies of Vitellius and Otho, rivals for the imperial throne, Otho being defeated. A few months later on the same field the army of Vitellius was overthrown by Vespasian, who succeeded him as emperor. Vitellius retired to Cremona, which was then placed under siege by Vespasian, and altho strongly fortified, captured.

205

THE BEST OF THE WORLD'S CLASSICS

blood, to whatever extent, were counterbalanced by the insatiable desire of plunder.

Antonius [29] determined upon the latter course, and ordered the rampart to be invested. The attack began at a distance with a volley of stones and darts, with the greater loss to the Flavians, on whom the enemy's weapons were thrown with advantage from above. Antonius presently assigned portions of the rampart and the gates to the legions that by this mode of attack in different quarters, valor and cowardice might be distinguished, and a spirit of emulation in honor animate the army. The third and seventh legions took their station nearest the road to Bedriacum; the seventh and eighth Claudian, a portion more to the right hand of the rampart; the thirteenth were carried by their own impetuosity to the gate that looked toward Brixia.[30] Some delay then took place while they supplied themselves from the neighboring villages with pickaxes, spades, and hooks, and scaling-ladders. They then formed a close military shell with their shields raised above their heads, and under that cover advanced to the ramparts. The Roman art of war was seen on both sides. The Vitellians rolled down massy stones, with which, having disjoined and shaken the shell, they inserted their long poles and spears; till at last, the whole frame and texture of the shields being dissolved, they strewed the ground with numbers of the crusht and mangled assailants. . . .

Severe in the extreme was the conflict main-

[29] Antonius Primus, the chief commander of Vespasian's forces.
[30] The modern Brescia.

tained by the third and the seventh legions. Antonius in person led on a select body of auxiliaries to the same quarter. The Vitellians were no longer able to sustain the shock of men all bent on victory, and seeing their darts fall on the military shell, and glide off without effect, at last they rolled down their battering-engine on the heads of the besiegers. For the moment, it dispersed and overwhelmed the party among which it fell; but it also drew after it, in its fall, the battlements and upper parts of the rampart. An adjoining tower, at the same time, yielded to the effect of stones which struck it, and left a breach, at which the seventh legion, in the form of a wedge, endeavored to force their way, while the third hewed down the gate with axes and swords. The first man that entered, according to all historians, was Caius Volusius, a common soldier of the third legion. He gained the summit of the rampart, and, bearing down all resistance, in the view of all beckoned with his hand, and cried aloud that the camp was captured. The rest of the legion followed him with resistless fury, the Vitellians being panic-struck, and throwing themselves headlong from the works. The whole space between the camp and the walls of Cremona was filled with slain.[31]

And now a new form of difficulty was presented by the high walls of the city, and towers of stone, the gates secured by iron bars, and troops brandishing their arms; the inhabitants, a large and numerous body, all devoted to Vitellius; and a conflux of people from all parts of

[31] According to Josephus 30,000 of the Vitellians perished and 4,500 of the followers of Vespasian.

Italy at the stated fair which was then held. The latter was regarded by the garrison as an aid, from the increase of numbers; but inflamed the ardor of the besiegers on the score of booty. Antonius ordered his men to take combustibles, and set fire to the most elegant edifices without the city; if, peradventure, the inhabitants, seeing their mansions destroyed, would be induced to abandon the adverse cause. In the houses that stood near the walls, of a height to overlook the works, he placed the bravest of his troops; and from those stations beams, tiles and firebrands were thrown down to drive the defenders of the walls from their posts.

The legions under Antonius now formed a military shell, while the rest poured in a volley of stones and darts; when the spirit of the besieged gradually gave way. The men highest in rank were willing to make terms for themselves, lest, if Cremona was taken by storm, they should receive no quarter, and the conquerors, disdaining vulgar lives, should fall on the tribunes and centurions, from whom the largest booty was to be expected. The common men, as usual, careless about future events, and safe in their obscurity, still held out. Roaming about the streets, or lurking in private houses, they did not sue for peace even when they had given up the contest. The principal officers took down the name and images of Vitellius. Cæcina, for he was still in confinement, they released from his fetters, and desired his aid in pleading their cause with the conqueror. He heard their petition with disdain, swelling with insolence, while they importuned him with tears; the last stage of human misery, when so many brave and gallant men were obliged to sue to a traitor for protection! They then hung out from the walls the fillets and badges of supplicants. When Antonius ordered a cessation of hostilities, the garrison brought out their eagles and standards; a mournful train of soldiers without their arms, their eyes riveted to the ground, followed them. The conquerors gathered round them, and first heaped reproaches upon them, and threatened violence to their persons; but afterward, when they saw the passiveness with which they received the insults, and that the vanquished, abandoning all their former pride, submitted to every indignity, the thought occurred that these very men lately conquered at Bedriacum, and used their victory with moderation. But when Cæcina came forth, decorated with his robes, and preceded by his lictors, who opened a way for him through the crowd, the indignation of the victors burst into a flame. They reproached him for his pride, his cruelty, and even for his treachery: so detested is villainy. Antonius opposed the fury of his men, and sent him under escort to Vespasian.

Meanwhile, the common people of Cremona, in the midst of so many soldiers, were subjected to grievous oppressions, and were in danger of being all put to the sword, if the rage of the soldiery had not been assuaged by the entreaties of their leaders. Antonius called them to an assembly, when he spoke of the conquerors in lofty terms, and of the vanquished with humanity; of Cremona he said nothing either way. But the army, adding to their love of plunder an inveterate aversion to the people, were bent on the extirpation of the inhabitants. In the war against Otho they were deemed the abettors of Vitellius; and afterward, when the thirteenth legion was left among them to build an amphitheater, with the usual insolence of the lower orders in towns, they had assailed them with offensive ribaldry. The spectacle of gladiators exhibited there by Cæcina inflamed the animosity against the people. Their city, too, was now for the second time the seat of war; and, in the heat of the last engagement, the Vitellians were thence supplied with refreshments; and some of their women, led into the field of battle by their zeal for the cause, were slain. The period, too, of the fair had given to a colony otherwise affluent an imposing appearance of accumulated wealth. Antonius, by his fame and brilliant success, eclipsed all the other commanders: the attention of all was fixt on him alone. He hastened to the baths to wash off the blood; and on observing that the water was not hot enough, he said that they would soon grow hotter. The expression was caught up: a casual word among slaves had the effect of throwing upon him the whole odium of having given a signal for setting fire to Cremona, which was already in flames.

Forty thousand armed men had poured into it. The number of drudges and camp-followers was still greater, and more abandoned to lust and cruelty. Neither age nor dignity served as a protection; deeds of lust were perpetrated amidst scenes of carnage, and murder was added to rape. Aged men and women that had passed their prime, and who were useless as booty, were made the objects of brutal sport. If a mature maiden, or any one of comely apearance, fell in their way, after being torn piecemeal by the rude hands of contending ruffians, they at last were the occasion of their turning their swords against each other. While eagerly carrying off money or massy gold from the temples, they were butchered by others stronger than themselves. Not content with the treasures that lay open to their view, some forced the owners to discover their hidden wealth, and dig up their buried riches. Numbers carried flaming torches, and, as soon as they had brought forth their booty, in their wanton sport set the gutted houses and plundered temples on fire. In an army differing in language and manners, composed of Roman citizens, allies, and foreign auxiliaries, all the diversities of passions were exhibited. Each had his separate notions of right and wrong; nor was anything unlawful. Four days did Cremona minister to their rapacity. When everything else, sacred and profane, was leveled in the conflagration, the temple of Memphitis alone remained standing, outside of the walls; saved either by its situation, or the influence of the deity.

Such was the fate of Cremona, two hundred and eighty-six years from its foundation. It was built during the consulship of Tiberius Sempronius and Publius Cornelius, at the time when Hannibal threatened an irruption into Italy, as a bulwark against the Gauls inhabiting beyond the Po, or any other power that might break in over the Alps. The colony, as might be expected, grew and flourished in the number of its settlers, from the contiguity of rivers, the fertility of its soil, from alliances and intermarriages with the neighboring people; never having suffered from foreign wars, but a sad sufferer from civil dissensions. Antonius, shrinking from the infamy of this horrible transaction (for the detestation it excited was increasing), issued an edict forbidding all manner of persons to detain the citizens of Cremona as prisoners of war. At the same time the booty was rendered valueless by a resolution adopted throughout Italy, not to purchase the captives taken on that occasion. The soldiers then began to murder them. However, when this was known, the prisoners were eagerly ransomed by their friends and relations. The survivors in a short time returned to Cremona. The temples and public places were rebuilt, at the recommendation of Vespasian, by the munificence of the burgesses.

VII

AGRICOLA[32]

CNÆUS JULIUS AGRICOLA was born at the ancient and illustrious colony of Forum Julii. Both his grandfathers were imperial procurators, an office which confers the rank of equestrian nobility. His father, Julius Græcinus, of the senatorian order, was famous for the study of eloquence and philosophy; and by these accomplishments he drew on himself the displeasure of Caius Cæsar,[33] for, being commanded to undertake the

[32] From the Oxford translation revised.
[33] Caligula, not Caius Julius Cæsar, is here referred to, he also having borne the name of Caius.

accusation of Marcus Silanus—on his refusal, he was put to death. His mother was Julia Procilla, a lady of exemplary chastity. Educated with tenderness in her bosom, he passed his childhood and youth in the attainment of every liberal art. He was preserved from the allurements of vice, not only by a naturally good disposition, but by being sent very early to pursue his studies at Massilia;[34] a place where Grecian politeness and provincial frugality are happily united. I remember he was used to relate, that in his early youth he should have engaged with more ardor in philosophical speculation than was suitable to a Roman and a senator, had not the prudence of his mother restrained the warmth and vehemence of his disposition: for his lofty and upright spirit, inflamed by the charms of glory and exalted reputation, led him to the pursuit with more eagerness than discretion. Reason and riper years tempered his warmth; and from the study of wisdom, he retained what is most difficult to compass—moderation.

He learned the rudiments of war in Britain, under Suetonius Paulinus, an active and prudent commander, who chose him for his tent companion, in order to form an estimate of his merit. Nor did Agricola, like many young men, who convert military service into wanton pastime, avail himself licentiously or slothfully of his tribunitial title, or his inexperience, to spend his time in pleasures and absences from duty; but he employed himself in gaining a knowledge of the

[34] Now Marseilles, founded by Phœnicians, who introduced, there a degree of Greek culture which long made the city famous.

country, making himself known to the army, learning from the experienced, and imitating the best; neither pressing to be employed through vainglory, nor declining it through timidity; and performing his duty with equal solicitude and spirit. At no other time in truth was Britain more agitated or in a state of greater uncertainty. Our veterans slaughtered, our colonies burned, our armies cut off—we were then contending for safety, afterward for victory. During this period, altho all things were transacted under the conduct and direction of another, and the stress of the whole, as well as the glory of recovering the province, fell to the general's share, yet they imparted to the young Agricola skill, experience, and incentives; and the passion for military glory entered his soul; a passion ungrateful to the times, in which eminence was unfavorably construed, and a great reputation was no less dangerous than a bad one.

Departing thence to undertake the offices of magistracy in Rome, he married Domitia Decidiana, a lady of illustrious descent, from which connection he derived credit and support in his pursuit of greater things. They lived together in admirable harmony and mutual affection; each giving the preference to the other; a conduct equally laudable in both, except that a greater degree of praise is due to a good wife, in proportion as a bad one deserves the greater censure. The lot of questorship gave him Asia for his province, and the proconsul Salvius Titianus[35] for his superior; by neither of which circumstances was he corrupted, altho the province was

[35] A brother of the Emperor Otho.

wealthy and open to plunder, and the proconsul, from his rapacious disposition, would readily have agreed to a mutual concealment of guilt. His family was there increased by the birth of a daughter, who was both the support of his house, and his consolation; for he lost an elder-born son in infancy. . . .

On his return from commanding the legion he was raised by Vespasian to the patrician order, and then invested with the government of Aquitania, a distinguished promotion, both in respect to the office itself, and the hopes of the consulate to which it destined him. It is a common supposition that military men, habituated to the unscrupulous and summary processes of camps, where things are carried with a strong hand, are deficient in the address and subtlety of genius requisite in civil jurisdiction. Agricola, however, by his natural prudence, was enabled to act with facility and precision even among civilians. He distinguished the hours of business from those of relaxation. When the court or tribunal demanded his presence, he was grave, intent, awful, yet generally inclined to lenity. When the duties of his office were over, the man of power was instantly laid aside. Nothing of sternness, arrogance, or rapaciousness appeared; and, what was a singular felicity, his affability did not impair his authority, nor his severity render him less beloved. To mention integrity and freedom from corruption in such a man, would be an affront to his virtues. He did not even court reputation, an object to which men of worth frequently sacrifice, by ostentation or artifice: equally avoiding competition with his colleagues, and contention with the procurators. To overcome in such a contest he thought inglorious; and to be put down, a disgrace. Somewhat less than three years were spent in this office, when he was recalled to the immediate prospect of the consulate; while at the same time a popular opinion prevailed that the government of Britain would be conferred upon him; an opinion not founded upon any suggestions of his own, but upon his being thought equal to the station. Common fame does not always err, sometimes it even directs a choice. When Consul,[36] he contracted his daughter, a lady already of the happiest promise, to myself, then a very young man; and after his office was expired I received her in marriage. He was immediately appointed governor of Britain, and the pontificate was added to his other dignities. . . .

His decease was a severe affliction to his family, a grief to his friends, and a subject of regret even to foreigners, and those who had no personal knowledge of him. The common people too, and the class who little interest themselves about public concerns, were frequent in their inquiries at his house during his sickness, and made him the subject of conversation at the forum and in private circles; nor did any person either rejoice at the news of his death, or speedily forget it. Their commiseration was aggravated by a prevailing report that he was taken off by poison. I can not venture to affirm anything certain of this matter; yet, during the whole course of his illness, the principal of the imperial

[36] Agricola was Consul in 77 A.D., and had for colleague Domitian, afterward Emperor.

freedmen and the most confidential of the physicians was sent much more frequently than was customary with a court whose visits were chiefly paid by messages; whether that was done out of real solicitude, or for the purposes of state inquisition. On the day of his decease, it is certain that accounts of his approaching dissolution were every instant transmitted to the emperor by couriers stationed for the purpose; and no one believed that the information, which so much pains was taken to accelerate, could be received with regret. He put on, however, in his countenance and demeanor, the semblance of grief: for he was now secured from an object of hatred, and could more easily conceal his joy than his fear. It was well known that on reading the will, in which he was nominated co-heir with the excellent wife and most dutiful daughter of Agricola, he exprest great satisfaction, as if it had been a voluntary testimony of honor and esteem: so blind and corrupt had his mind been rendered by continual adulation, that he was ignorant none but a bad prince could be nominated heir to a good father.

PLINY THE YOUNGER

Born at Como, in 63 A.D.; died in 113; nephew of the elder Pliny; Consul in 100; governor of Bithynia and Pontus in 111; friend of Trajan and Tacitus; his letters and a eulogy of Trajan alone among his writings have survived.

I

OF THE CHRISTIANS IN HIS PROVINCE [1]

It is my invariable rule, Sir, to refer to you in all matters where I feel doubtful; for who is more capable of removing my scruples, or informing my ignorance? Having never been present at any trials concerning those who profess Christianity, I am unacquainted not only with the nature of their crimes, or the measure of their punishment, but how far it is proper to enter into an examination concerning them. Whether, therefore, any difference is usually made with respect to ages, or no distinction is to be observed between the young and the adult; whether repentance entitles them to a pardon;

[1] Addrest to the Emperor Trajan while proconsul in Pontus and Bithynia. The Melmoth translation revised by Bosanquet. This letter, and the passage in Tacitus printed elsewhere in this volume, are the only genuine contemporary references to the early Christians to be found in ancient writings. Pliny's letter was preserved by the Christians themselves as evidence of the purity of their faith and practises. Early writers of the Church frequently appealed to it against calumniators. It was written within forty years of the death of St. Paul.

218

or if a man has been once a Christian, it avails nothing to desist from his error; whether the very profession of Christianity, unattended with any criminal act, or only the crimes themselves inherent in the profession are punishable; on all these points I am in great doubt. In the meanwhile, the method I have observed toward those who have been brought before me as Christians is this: I asked them whether they were Christians; if they admitted it, I repeated the question twice, and threatened them with punishment; if they persisted, I ordered them to be at once punished: for I was persuaded whatever the nature of their opinions might be, a contumacious and inflexible obstinacy certainly deserved correction. There were others also brought before me possest with the same infatuation, but being Roman citizens I directed them to be sent to Rome.

But this crime spreading (as is usually the case) while it was actually under prosecution, several instances of the same nature occurred. An anonymous information was laid before me, containing a charge against several persons, who upon examination denied they were Christians, or had ever been so. They repeated after me an invocation to the gods, and offered religious rites with wine and incense before your statue (which for that purpose I had ordered to be brought, together with those of the gods), and even reviled the name of Christ: whereas there is no forcing, it is said, those who are really Christians into any of these compliances: I thought it proper, therefore, to discharge them. Some among those who were accused by a witness in person at first confest themselves Christians but immediately after denied it; the rest owned indeed that they had been of that number formerly, but had now (some above three, others more, and a few above twenty years ago) renounced that error. They all worshiped your statue and the images of the gods, uttering imprecations at the same time against the name of Christ. They affirmed the whole of their guilt, or their error, was, that they met on a stated day before it was light, and addrest a form of prayer to Christ, as to a divinity, binding themselves by a solemn oath, not for the purposes of any wicked design, but never to commit any fraud, theft, or adultery, never to falsify their word, nor deny a trust when they should be called upon to deliver it up; after which it was their custom to separate, and then reassemble, to eat in common a harmless meal. From this custom, however, they desisted after the publication of my edict, by which, according to your commands, I forbade the meeting of any assemblies.

After receiving this account, I judged it so much the more necessary to endeavor to extort the real truth by putting two female slaves to the torture, who were said to officiate in their religious rites: but all I could discover was evidence of an absurd and extravagant superstition. I deemed it expedient, therefore, to adjourn all further proceedings, in order to consult you. For it appears to be a matter highly deserving your consideration, more especially as great numbers must be involved in the danger of these prosecutions, which have already extended, and are still likely to extend, to persons of all ranks and ages, and even of both sexes.

PLINY THE YOUNGER

In fact, this contagious superstition is not confined to the cities only, but has spread its infection among the neighboring villages and country. Nevertheless, it still seems possible to restrain its progress. The temples, at least, which were once almost deserted, begin now to be frequented; and the sacred rites after a long intermission, are again revived; while there is a general demand for the victims, which till lately found very few purchasers. From all this it is easy to conjecture what numbers might be reclaimed if a general pardon were granted to those who shall repent of their error.[2]

[2] Trajan's reply to this letter was as follows: "You have adopted the right course, my dearest Secundus, in investigating the charges against the Christians who were brought before you. It is not possible to lay down any general rule for all such cases. Do not go out of your way to look for them. If indeed they should be brought before you, and the crime is proved, they must be punished; with the restriction, however, that where the party denies he is a Christian, and shall make it evident that he is not, by invoking our gods, let him (notwithstanding any former suspicion) be pardoned upon his repentance. Anonymous informations ought not to be received in any sort of prosecution. It is introducing a very dangerous precedent, and is quite foreign to the spirit of our age."

II

TO TACITUS ON THE ERUPTION OF VESUVIUS[3]
(79 A.D.)

Your request that I would send you an account of my uncle's[4] death, in order to transmit a more exact relation of it to posterity, deserves my acknowledgments; for, if this accident shall be celebrated by your pen, the glory of it, I am well assured, will be rendered forever illustrious. And notwithstanding he perished by a misfortune, which, as it involved at the same time a most beautiful country in ruins, and destroyed so many populous cities, seems to promise him an everlasting remembrance; notwithstanding he has himself composed many and lasting works; yet I am persuaded the mentioning of him in your immortal writings will greatly contribute to render his name immortal.

He was at that time with the fleet under his command at Misenum.[5] On the 24th of August, about one in the afternoon, my mother desired him to observe a cloud which appeared of a very unusual size and shape. He had just taken a

---

[3] The translation of William Melmoth, revised by F. C. T. Bosanquet. Pliny wrote two letters to Tacitus on this subject, each at the request of the historian. Both are given here.

[4] Pliny the Elder was his uncle.

[5] In the Bay of Naples.

PLINY THE YOUNGER

turn in the sun, and, after bathing himself in cold water, and making a light luncheon, gone back to his books: he immediately arose and went out upon a rising ground from whence he might get a better sight of this very uncommon appearance. A cloud, from which mountain was uncertain, at this distance (but it was found afterward to come from Mount Vesuvius),[*] was ascending, the appearance of which I can not give you a more exact description of than by likening it to that of a pine-tree, for it shot up to a great height in the form of a very tall trunk, which spread itself out at the top into a sort of branches; occasioned, I imagine, either by a sudden gust of air that impelled it, the force of which decreased as it advanced upward, or the cloud itself being prest back again by its own weight, expanded in the manner I have mentioned; it appeared sometimes bright and sometimes dark and spotted according as it was either more or less impregnated with earth and cinders. This phenomenon seemed to a man of such learning and research as my uncle extraordinary and worth further looking into. He ordered a light vessel to be got ready, and gave me leave, if I liked, to accompany him. I said I had rather go on with my work; and it so happened he had himself given me something to write out.

As he was coming out of the house, he received a note from Rectina, the wife of Bassus, who was in the utmost alarm at the imminent danger which threatened her; for her villa lying at the

[*] About six miles distant from Naples. This eruption of Vesuvius, in which Herculaneum and Pompeii were buried, happened A.D. 79, in the first year of the emperor Titus.

223

foot of Mount Vesuvius, there was no way of escape but by sea; she earnestly entreated him therefore to come to her assistance. He accordingly changed his first intention and what he had begun from a philosophical, he now carries out in a noble and generous spirit. He ordered the galleys to put to sea and went himself on board with an intention of assisting not only Rectina, but the several other towns which lay thickly strewn along that beautiful coast. Hastening then to the place from whence others fled with the utmost terror, he steered his course direct to the point of danger, and with so much calmness and presence of mind as to be able to make and dictate his observations upon the motion and all the phenomena of that dreadful scene. He was now so close to the mountain that the cinders, which grew thicker and hotter the nearer he approached, fell into the ships, together with pumice stones, and black pieces of burning rock: they were in danger too not only of being aground by the sudden retreat of the sea, but also from the vast fragments which rolled down from the mountains, and obstructed all the shore. Here he stopt to consider whether he should turn back again; to which the pilot advising him, "Fortune," said he, "favors the brave; steer to where Pomponianus is." Pomponianus was then at Stabiæ,[7] separated by a bay, which the sea, after several insensible windings, forms with the shore. He had already sent his baggage on board; for tho he was not at that time in actual danger, yet being within sight of it, and indeed

[7] Now called Castellammare, in the Bay of Naples, about fifteen miles southeast of the city of Naples.

extremely near, if it should in the least increase, he was determined to put to sea as soon as the wind, which was blowing dead in-shore, should go down.

It was favorable, however, for carrying my uncle to Pomponianus, whom he found in the greatest consternation: he embraced him tenderly, encouraging and urging him to keep up his spirits, and the more effectually to soothe his fears by seeming unconcerned himself, ordered a bath to be got ready, and then, after having bathed, sat down to supper with great cheerfulness, or at least (what is just as heroic) with every appearance of it. Meanwhile broad flames shone out in several places from Mount Vesuvius, which the darkness of the night contributed to render still brighter and clearer. But my uncle, in order to soothe the apprehensions of his friend, assured him it was only the burning of the villages, which the country people had abandoned to the flames: after this he retired to rest, and it is most certain he was so little disquieted as to fall into a sound sleep: for his breathing, which, on account of his corpulence, was rather heavy and sonorous, was heard by the attendants outside. The court which led to his apartment being now almost filled with stones and ashes, if he had continued there any time longer, it would have been impossible for him to have made his way out. So he was awoke and got up, and went to Pomponianus and the rest of his company, who were feeling too anxious to think of going to bed. They consulted together whether it would be most prudent to trust to the houses, which now rocked from side to side with frequent and violent concussions as tho shaken from their very foundations; or fly to the open fields, where the calcined stones and cinders, tho light indeed, yet fell in large showers, and threatened destruction. In this choice of dangers they resolved for the fields: a resolution which, while the rest of the company were hurried into by their fears, my uncle embraced upon cool and deliberate consideration. They went out then, having pillows tied upon their heads with napkins; and this was their whole defense against the storm of stones that fell round them.

It was now day everywhere else, but there a deeper darkness prevailed than in the thickest night; which however was in some degree alleviated by torches and other lights of various kinds. They thought proper to go farther down upon the shore to see if they might safely put out to sea, but found the waves still running extremely high, and boisterous. There my uncle, laying himself down upon a sail-cloth, which was spread for him, called twice for some cold water, which he drank, when immediately the flames, preceded by a strong whiff of sulfur, dispersed the rest of the party, and obliged him to rise. He raised himself up with the assistance of two of his servants, and instantly fell down dead; suffocated, as I conjecture, by some gross and noxious vapor, having always had a weak throat, which was often inflamed. As soon as it was light again, which was not till the third day after this melancholy accident, his body was found entire, and without any marks of violence upon it, in the dress in which he fell, and looking more like a man asleep than dead. . . .

PLINY THE YOUNGER

My uncle having left us,[8] I spent such time as was left on my studies (it was on their account indeed that I had stopt behind), till it was time for my bath. After which I went to supper, and then fell into a short and uneasy sleep. There had been noticed for many days before a trembling of the earth, which did not alarm us much, as this is quite an ordinary occurrence in Campania; but it was so particularly violent that night that it not only shook but actually overturned, as it would seem, everything about us. My mother rushed into my chamber, where she found me rising, in order to awaken her. We sat down in the open court of the house, which occupied a small space between the buildings and the sea. As I was at that time but eighteen years of age, I know not whether I should call my behavior, in this dangerous juncture, courage or folly; but I took up Livy, and amused myself with turning over that author, and even making extracts from him, as if I had been perfectly at my leisure. Just then, a friend of my uncle's, who had lately come to him from Spain, joined us, and observing me sitting by my mother with a book in my hand, reproved her for her calmness, and me at the same time for my careless security: nevertheless I went on with my author.

Tho it was now morning, the light was still exceedingly faint and doubtful; the buildings all around us tottered, and tho we stood upon open ground, yet as the place was narrow and confined, there was no remaining without imminent danger: we therefore resolved to quit the town.

[8] The paragraphs from this point to the end are from Pliny's second letter to Tacitus.

A panic-stricken crowd followed us, and (as to a mind distracted with terror every suggestion seems more prudent than its own) prest on us in dense array to drive us forward as we came out. Being at a convenient distance from the houses, we stood still, in the midst of a most dangerous and dreadful scene. The chariots, which we had ordered to be drawn out, were so agitated backward and forward, tho upon the most level ground, that we could not keep them steady, even by supporting them with large stones. The sea seemed to roll back upon itself, and to be driven from its banks by the convulsive motion of the earth; it is certain at least the shore was considerably enlarged, and several sea animals were left upon it. On the other side, a black and dreadful cloud, broken with rapid, zigzag flashes, revealed behind it variously shaped masses of flame: these last were like sheet-lightning, but much larger. Upon this our Spanish friend, whom I mentioned above, addressing himself to my mother and me with great energy and urgency: "If your brother," he said, "if your uncle be safe, he certainly wishes you may be so too; but if he perished, it was his desire, no doubt, that you might both survive him: why therefore do you delay your escape a moment?" We could never think of our own safety, we said, while we were uncertain of his. Upon this our friend left us, and withdrew from the danger with the utmost precipitation. Soon afterward, the cloud began to descend, and cover the sea. It had already surrounded and concealed the island of Capreæ.*

* The island near Naples, now called Capri.

PLINY THE YOUNGER

My mother now besought, urged, even commanded me to make my escape at any rate, which, as I was young, I might easily do; as for herself, she said, her age and corpulency rendered all attempts of that sort impossible; however she would willingly meet death if she could have the satisfaction of seeing that she was not the occasion of mine. But I absolutely refused to leave her, and, taking her by the hand, compelled her to go with me. She complied with great reluctance, and not without many reproaches to herself for retarding my flight. The ashes now began to fall upon us, tho in no great quantity. I looked back; a dense dark mist seemed to be following us, spreading itself over the country like a cloud. "Let us turn out of the high-road," I said, "while we can still see, for fear that, should we fall in the road, we should be prest to death in the dark, by the crowds that are following us." We had scarcely sat down when night came upon us, not such as we have when the sky is cloudy, or when there is no moon, but that of a room when it is shut up, and all the lights put out. You might hear the shrieks of women, the screams of children, and the shouts of men; some calling for their children, others for their parents, others for their husbands, and seeking to recognize each other by the voices that replied; one lamenting his own fate, another that of his family; some wishing to die, from the very fear of dying; some lifting their hands to the gods; but the greater part convinced that there were now no gods at all, and that the final endless night of which we have heard had come upon the world. Among these there were some who augmented the real terrors by others imaginary or wilfully invented. I remember some who declared that one part of Misenum had fallen, that another was on fire; it was false, but they found people to believe them. It now grew rather lighter, which we imagined to be rather the forerunner of an approaching burst of flames (as in truth it was) than the return of day: however, the fire fell at a distance from us: then again we were immersed in thick darkness, and a heavy shower of ashes rained upon us, which we were obliged every now and then to stand up to shake off, otherwise we should have been crusht and buried in the heap.

I might boast that, during all this scene of horror, not a sigh, or expression of fear, escaped me, had not my support been grounded in that miserable, tho mighty, consolation, that all mankind were involved in the same calamity and that I was perishing with the world itself. At last this dreadful darkness was dissipated by degrees, like a cloud or smoke; the real day returned, and even the sun shone out, tho with a lurid light, like when an eclipse is coming on. Every object that presented itself to our eyes (which were extremely weakened) seemed changed, being covered deep with ashes as if with snow. My mother and I, notwithstanding the danger we had passed, and that which still threatened us, had no thoughts of leaving the place, till we could receive some news of my uncle.

SUETONIUS

Lived in the first half of the second century A.D.; biographer and historian; private secretary of the emperor Hadrian about 119-121; a friend of the younger Pliny, whom he accompanied to Bithynia in 112; wrote several works, of which only his "Lives of the Twelve Cæsars" have survived.

I

THE LAST DAYS OF AUGUSTUS[1]
(14 A.D.)

His death, of which I shall now speak, and his subsequent deification, were intimated by divers manifest prodigies. As he was finishing the census amidst a great crowd of people in the Campus Martius, an eagle hovered round him several times, and then directed its course to a neighboring temple, where it settled upon the name of Agrippa, and at the first letter. Upon observing this, he ordered his colleague Tiberius to put up the vows, which it is usual to make on such occasions, for the succeeding Lustrum. For he declared he would not meddle with what it was probable he should never accomplish, tho the tables were ready drawn for it. About the same time, the first letter of his name, in an inscription upon one of his statues, was struck out by lightning; which was interpreted as a presage that he would live only a hundred days

[1] From the translation by Alexander Thomson, revised by T. Forester.

longer, the letter C denoting that number; and that he would be placed among the gods as Æsar, which in the remaining part of the word Cæsar, signifies, in the Tuscan language, a god. Being, therefore, about dispatching Tiberius to Illyricum, and designing to go with him as far as Beneventum, but being detained by several persons who applied to him respecting causes they had depending, he cried out (and it was afterward regarded as an omen of his death), "Not all the business in the world shall detain me at Rome one moment longer"; and setting out upon his journey, he went as far as Astura, whence, contrary to his custom, he put to sea in the night-time, as there was a favorable wind.

His malady proceeded from diarrhea; notwithstanding which, he went round the coast of Campania, and the adjacent islands, and spent four days in that of Capri; where he gave himself up entirely to repose and relaxation. Happening to sail by the bay of Puteoli,[2] the passengers and mariners aboard a ship of Alexandria, just then arrived, clad all in white, with chaplets upon their heads, and offering incense, loaded him with praises and joyful acclamations, crying out, "By you we live, by you we sail securely, by you enjoy our liberty and our fortunes." At which being greatly pleased, he distributed to each of those who attended him, forty gold pieces, requiring from them an assurance on oath, not to employ the sum given them in

[2] Now Pozzuoli, which fronts on the bay, seven miles west of Naples. It still has ruins of an amphitheater, 482 feet by 384 in size. In Roman times it was an important commercial city.

any other way than the purchase of Alexandrian merchandise. And during several days afterward, he distributed Togæ and Pallia, among other gifts, on condition that the Romans should use the Greek and the Greeks the Roman dress and language. He likewise constantly attended to see the boys perform their exercises, according to an ancient custom still continued at Capri. He gave them likewise an entertainment in his presence, and not only permitted, but required from them the utmost freedom in jesting, and scrambling for fruit, victuals, and other things which he threw among them. In a word, he indulged himself in all the ways of amusement he could contrive. . . .

Upon the day of his death, he now and then inquired if there was any disturbance in the town on his account; and calling for a mirror, he ordered his hair to be combed, and his shrunk cheeks to be adjusted. Then asking his friends who were admitted into the room, "Do ye think that I have acted my part on the stage of life well?" he immediately subjoined,

"If all be right, with joy your voices raise,
In loud applauses to the actor's praise."

After which, having dismissed them all, whilst he was inquiring of some persons who were just arrived from Rome, concerning Drusus's daughter, who was in a bad state of health, he expired suddenly, amidst the kisses of Livia, and with these words: "Livia! live mindful of our union; and now, farewell!" dying a very easy death, and such as he himself had always wished for. For as often as he heard that any person had died quickly and without pain, he wished for himself and his friends the like *euthanasia* (an easy death), for that was the word he made use of. He betrayed but one symptom, before he breathed his last, of being delirious, which was this: he was all on a sudden much frightened, and complained that he was carried away by forty men. But this was rather a presage, than any delirium: for precisely that number of soldiers, belonging to the prætorian cohort, carried out his corpse.

He expired in the same room in which his father Octavius had died, when the two Sextus's, Pompey and Apuleius, were Consuls, upon the fourteenth of the calends of September [the 19th August], at the ninth hour of the day, being seventy-six years of age, wanting only thirty-five days. His remains were carried by the magistrates of the municipal towns and colonies, from Nola to Bovillæ,[3] and in the night-time because of the season of the year. During the intervals, the body lay in some basilica, or great temple, of each town. At Bovillæ it was met by the Equestrian Order, who carried it to the city, and deposited it in the vestibule of his own house. The senate proceeded with so much zeal in the arrangement of his funeral, and paying honor to his memory, that, among several other proposals, some were for having the funeral procession made through the triumphal gate, preceded by the image of Victory which is in the senate-house, and the children of highest rank and of both sexes singing the funeral dirge. Others

[3] Bovillæ is now known as Frattochio. It stands on the Appian Way, about nineteen miles from Rome.

proposed, that on the day of the funeral, they should lay aside their gold rings, and wear rings of iron; and others, that his bones should be collected by the priests of the principal colleges. One likewise proposed to transfer the name of August to September, because he was born in the latter, but died in the former. Another moved, that the whole period of time, from his birth to his death, should be called the Augustan age, and be inserted in the calendar under that title. But at last it was judged proper to be moderate in the honors paid to his memory. Two funeral orations were pronounced in his praise, one before the temple of Julius, by Tiberius; and the other before the rostra, under the old shops, by Drusus, Tiberius's son. The body was then carried upon the shoulders of senators into the Campus Martius, and there burned. A man of prætorian rank affirmed upon oath, that he saw his spirit ascend from the funeral pile to heaven. The most distinguished persons of the equestrian order, barefooted, and with their tunics loose, gathered up his relics, and deposited them in the mausoleum[*] which had been built in his sixth consulship between the Flaminian Way and the bank of the Tiber; at which time likewise he gave the groves and walks about it for the use of the people.

[*] This mausoleum was of white marble rising in terraces to a great height, and was crowned by a dome on which stood a statue of Augustus. Marcellus was the first person buried there. Its site was near the present Porta del Popolo.

II

THE GOOD DEEDS OF NERO[5]

HE was seventeen years of age at the death of that prince,[6] and as soon as that event was made public, he went out to the cohort on guard between the hours of six and seven; for the omens were so disastrous, that no earlier time of the day was judged proper. On the steps before the palace gate, he was unanimously saluted by the soldiers as their emperor, and then carried in a litter to the camp; thence, after making a short speech to the troops, into the senate-house, where he continued until the evening; of all the immense honors which were heaped upon him, refusing none but the title of FATHER OF HIS COUNTRY, on account of his youth.

He began his reign with an ostentation of dutiful regard to the memory of Claudius, whom he buried with the utmost pomp and magnificence, pronouncing the funeral oration himself, and then had him enrolled among the gods. He paid likewise the highest honors to the memory of his father Domitius. He left the management of affairs, both public and private, to his mother. The word which he gave the first day of his reign to the tribune on guard was, "The Best of Mothers," and afterward he frequently appeared with her in the streets of Rome in her

[5] From the translation by Alexander Thomson, revised by T. Forester.
[6] The Emperor Claudius.

SUETONIUS

litter. He settled a colony at Antium,[7] in which he placed the veteran soldiers belonging to the guards; and obliged several of the richest centurions of the first rank to transfer their residence to that place; where he likewise made a noble harbor at a prodigious expense.

To establish still further his character, he declared, "that he designed to govern according to the model of Augustus"; and omitted no opportunity of showing his generosity, clemency, and complaisance. The more burdensome taxes he either entirely took off, or diminished. The rewards appointed for informers by the Papian law, he reduced to a fourth part, and distributed to the people four hundred sesterces a man. To the noblest of the senators who were much reduced in their circumstances, he granted annual allowances, in some cases as much as five hundred thousand sesterces; and to the prætorian cohorts a monthly allowance of corn gratis. When called upon to subscribe the sentence, according to custom, of a criminal condemned to die, "I wish," said he, "I had never learned to read and write." He continually saluted people of the several orders by name, without a prompter. When the senate returned him their thanks for his good government, he replied to them, "It will be time enough to do so when I shall have deserved it." He admitted the common people to see him perform his exercises in the Campus Martius. He frequently declaimed in public, and recited verses of his own com-

[7] Nero was born in Antium, distant from Rome about thirty-eight miles. The Apollo Belvidere was found among its ruins.

posing, not only at home, but in the theater; so much to the joy of all the people, that public prayers were appointed to be put up to the gods upon that account; and the verses which had been publicly read, were, after being written in gold letters, consecrated to Jupiter Capitolinus.

He presented the people with a great number and variety of spectacles, as the Juvenal and Circensian games, stage-plays, and an exhibition of gladiators. In the Juvenal, he even admitted senators and aged matrons to perform parts. In the Circensian games, he assigned the equestrian order seats apart from the rest of the people, and had races performed by chariots drawn each by four camels. In the games which he instituted for the eternal duration of the empire, and therefore ordered to be called *Maximi*, many of the senatorian and equestrian order, of both sexes, performed. A distinguished Roman knight descended on the stage by a rope, mounted on an elephant. A Roman play, likewise, composed by Afranius, was brought upon the stage. It was entitled, "The Fire"; and in it the performers were allowed to carry off, and to keep to themselves, the furniture of the house, which as the plot of the play required, was burned down in the theater. Every day during the solemnity, many thousand articles of all descriptions were thrown among the people to scramble for; such as fowls of different kinds, tickets for corn, clothes, gold, silver, gems, pearls, pictures, slaves, beasts of burden, wild beasts that had been tamed; at last, ships, lots of houses, and lands, were offered as prizes in a lottery.

These games he beheld from the front of the

SUETONIUS

proscenium. In the show of gladiators, which he exhibited in a wooden amphitheater, built within a year in the district of the Campus Martius, he ordered that none should be slain, not even the condemned criminals employed in the combats. He secured four hundred senators, and six hundred Roman knights, among whom were some of unbroken fortunes and unblemished reputation, to act as gladiators. From the same orders, he engaged persons to encounter wild beasts, and for various other services in the theater. He presented the public with the representation of a naval fight, upon sea-water, with huge fishes swimming in it; as also with the Pyrrhic dance, performed by certain youths, to each of whom, after the performance was over, he granted the freedom of Rome. During this diversion, a bull covered Pasiphaë, concealed within a wooden statue of a cow, as many of the spectators believed. Icarus, upon his first attempt to fly, fell on the stage close to the emperor's pavilion, and bespattered him with blood. For he very seldom presided in the games, but used to view them reclining on a couch, at first through some narrow apertures, but afterward with the *Podium* quite open. He was the first who instituted, in imitation of the Greeks, a trial of skill in the three several exercises of music, wrestling, and horse-racing, to be performed at Rome every five years, and which he called Neronia. Upon the dedication of his bath [8] and gymnasium, he furnished the senate and the equestrian order with oil. He appointed as judges of the trial men of consular

---
[8] These baths stood west of the Pantheon. Altho of great extent, no remains of them now exist.

rank, chosen by lot, who sat with the prætors. At this time he went down into the orchestra among the senators, and received the crown for the best performance in Latin prose and verse, for which several persons of the greatest merit contended, but they unanimously yielded to him. The crown for the best performer on the harp, being likewise awarded to him by the judges, he devoutly saluted it, and ordered it to be carried to the statue of Augustus. In the gymnastic exercises, which he presented in the Septa, while they were preparing the great sacrifice of an ox, he shaved his beard for the first time, and putting it up in a casket of gold studded with pearls of great price, consecrated it to Jupiter Capitolinus. He invited the Vestal Virgins to see the wrestlers perform, because, at Olympia, the priestesses of Ceres are allowed the privilege of witnessing that exhibition. . . .

Twice only he undertook any foreign expeditions, one to Alexandria, and the other to Achaia; but he abandoned the prosecution of the former on the very day fixt for his departure, by being deterred both by ill omens, and the hazard of the voyage. For while he was making the circuit of the temples, having seated himself in that of Vesta, when he attempted to rise, the skirt of his robe stuck fast; and he was instantly seized with such a dimness in his eyes, that he could not see a yard before him. In Achaia, he attempted to make a cut through the Isthmus;[*] and, having made a speech encouraging his pre-

[*] This scheme, which was a favorite one of many Roman emperors and even of Julius Cæsar, was not realized until our time. The Corinth canal was completed in 1893.

torians to set about the work, on a signal given by sound of trumpet, he first broke ground with a spade, and carried off a basketful of earth upon his shoulders. He made preparations for an expedition to the Pass of the Caspian mountains, forming a new legion out of his late levies in Italy, of men all six feet high, which he called the phalanx of Alexander the Great. These transactions, in part unexceptionable, and in part highly commendable, I have brought into one view, in order to separate them from the scandalous and criminal part of his conduct.

III

THE DEATH OF NERO[10]
(68 A.D.)

HE was terrified with manifest warnings, both old and new, arising from dreams, auspices, and omens. He had never been used to dream before the murder of his mother. After that event, he fancied in his sleep that he was steering a ship, and that the rudder was forced from him: that he was dragged by his wife Octavia into a prodigiously dark place; and was at one time covered over with a vast swarm of winged ants, and at another, surrounded by the national images which were set up near Pompey's theater, and hindered from advancing farther; that a

[10] From the translation by Alexander Thomson, revised by T. Forester.

Spanish jennet he was fond of, had his hinder parts so changed as to resemble those of an ape; and that having his head only left unaltered, he neighed very harmoniously. The doors of the mausoleum of Augustus flying open of themselves, there issued from it a voice, calling on him by name. The Lares being adorned with fresh garlands on the calends (the first) of January, fell down during the preparations for sacrificing to them. While he was taking the omens, Sporus presented him with a ring, the stone of which had carved upon it the Rape of Proserpine. When a great multitude of several orders was assembled, to attend at the solemnity of making vows to the gods, it was a long time before the keys of the Capitol could be found. And when, in a speech of his to the senate against Vindex, these words were read, "that the miscreants should be punished and soon make the end they merited," they all cried out, "You will do it, Augustus." It was likewise remarked, that the last tragic piece which he sung, was Œdipus in Exile, and that he fell as he was repeating this verse:

"Wife, mother, father, force me to my end."

Meanwhile, on the arrival of the news that the rest of the armies had declared against him, he tore to piece the letters which were delivered to him at dinner, overthrew the table, and dashed with violence against the ground two favorite cups, which he called Homer's, because some of that poet's verses were cut upon them. Then taking from Locusta a dose of poison, which he put up in a golden box, he went into the Ser-

SUETONIUS

vilian gardens, and thence dispatching a trusty freedman to Ostia, with orders to make ready a fleet, he endeavored to prevail with some tribunes and centurions of the prætorian guards to attend him in his flight; but part of them showing no great inclination to comply, others absolutely refusing, and one of them crying out aloud,

"Say, is it then so sad a thing to die?"

he was in great perplexity whether he should submit himself to Galba,[11] or apply to the Parthians for protection, or else appear before the people drest in mourning, and, upon the rostra, in the most piteous manner, beg pardon for his past misdemeanors, and, if he could not prevail, request of them to grant him at least the government of Egypt. A speech to this purpose was afterward found in his writing-case. But it is conjectured that he durst not venture upon this project, for fear of being torn to pieces, before he could get to the forum.

Deferring, therefore, his resolution until the next day, he awoke about midnight, and finding the guards withdrawn, he leapt out of bed, and sent round for his friends. But none of them vouchsafing any message in reply, he went with a few attendants to their houses. The doors being everywhere shut, and no one giving him any answer, he returned to his bed-chamber; whence those who had the charge of it had all now eloped; some having gone one way, and some another, carrying off with them his bedding

[11] The Roman general, then leader of the revolt against Nero, who was afterward proclaimed Emperor.

and box of poison. He then endeavored to find Spicillus, the gladiator, or some one to kill him; but not being able to procure any one, "What!" said he, "have I then neither friend nor foe?" and immediately ran out, as if he would throw himself into the Tiber.

But this furious impulse subsiding, he wished for some place of privacy, where he might collect his thoughts; and his freedman Phaon offering him his country-house, between the Salarian and Nomentan roads, about four miles from the city, he mounted a horse, barefoot as he was, and in his tunic, only slipping over it an old soiled cloak; with his head muffled up, and a handkerchief before his face, and four persons only to attend him, of whom Sporus was one. He was suddenly struck with horror by an earthquake, and by a flash of lightning which darted full in his face, and heard from the neighboring camp the shouts of the soldiers, wishing his destruction, and prosperity to Galba. He also heard a traveler they met on the road, say, "They are in pursuit of Nero": and another ask, "Is there any news in the city about Nero?" Uncovering his face when his horse was started by the scent of a carcass which lay in the road, he was recognized and saluted by an old soldier who had been discharged from the guards. When they came to the lane which turned up to the house, they quitted their horses, and with much difficulty he wound among bushes and briars, and along a track through a bed of rushes, over which they spread their cloaks for him to walk on. Having reached a wall at the back of the villa, Phaon advised him to hide himself a while in a sand-pit; when he replied, "I will not go underground alive." Staying there some little time, while preparations were made for bringing him privately into the villa, he took up some water out of a neighboring tank in his hand, to drink, saying, "This is Nero's distilled water." Then his cloak having been torn by the brambles, he pulled out the thorns which stuck in it. At last, being admitted, creeping upon his hands and knees, through a hole made for him in the wall, he lay down in the first closet he came to, upon a miserable pallet, with an old coverlet thrown over it; and being both hungry and thirsty, tho he refused some coarse bread that was brought him, he drank a little warm water.

All who surrounded him now pressing him to save himself from the indignities which were ready to befall him, he ordered a pit to be sunk before his eyes, of the size of his body, and the bottom to be covered with pieces of marble put together, if any could be found about the house; and water and wood to be got ready for immediate use about his corpse; weeping at everything that was done, and frequently saying, "What an artist is now about to perish!" Meanwhile, letters being brought in by a servant belonging to Phaon, he snatched them out of his hand, and there read, "That he had been declared an enemy by the senate, and that search was making for him, that he might be punished according to the ancient custom of the Romans." He then inquired what kind of punishment that was; and being told, that the practise was to strip the criminal naked, and scourge him to death while his neck was fastened within a forked stake, he was so terrified that he took up two daggers which he had brought with him, and after feeling the points of both, put them up again, saying, "The fatal hour is not yet come." One while, he begged of Sporus to begin to wail and lament; another while, he entreated that one of them would set him an example by killing himself; and then again, he condemned his own want of resolution in these words: "I yet live to my shame and disgrace: this is not becoming for Nero: it is not becoming. Thou oughtest in such circumstances to have a good heart: Come then: courage, man!" The horsemen who had received orders to bring him away alive, were now approaching the house. As soon as he heard them coming, he uttered with a trembling voice the following verse,

"The noise of swift-heel'd steeds assails my ears";

he drove a dagger into his throat, being assisted in the act by Epaphroditus,[12] his secretary. A centurion bursting in just as he was half-dead, and applying his cloak to the wound, pretending that he was come to his assistance, he made no other reply but this, "'Tis too late"; and "Is this your loyalty?" Immediately after pronouncing these words, he expired, with his eyes fixt and starting out of his head, to the terror of all who beheld him. . . .

In stature he was a little below the common height; his skin was foul and spotted; his hair inclined to yellow; his features were agreeable,

[12] Epaphroditus was the master of Epictetus, the Stoic philosopher, before his freedom.

rather than handsome; his eyes gray and dull, his neck was thick, his belly prominent, his legs very slender, his constitution sound. For, tho excessively luxurious in his mode of living, he had, in the course of fourteen years, only three fits of sickness; which were so slight, that he neither forbore the use of wine, nor made any alteration in his usual diet. In his dress, and the care of his person, he was so careless, that he had his hair cut in rings, one above another; and when in Achaia, he let it grow long behind; and he generally appeared in public in the loose dress which he used at table, with a handkerchief about his neck and without either a girdle or shoes.

MARCUS AURELIUS

Born in Rome in 121 A.D.; died in 180; celebrated as emperor and Stoic philosopher; a nephew of Antoninus Pius, whom he succeeded as emperor, with Lucius Verus; after the death of Verus in 169 became sole emperor; his reign notable for wisdom and the happiness of the Roman people; wrote his "Meditations" in Greek; a bronze equestrain statue of him in Rome is the finest extant specimen of ancient bronze.

HIS DEBT TO OTHERS[1]

1. From my grandfather Verus[2] [I learned] good morals and the government of my temper.

2. From the reputation and remembrance of my father,[3] modesty and a manly character.

3. From my mother,[4] piety and beneficence, and abstinence, not only from evil deeds, but even from evil thoughts; and, further, simplicity in my way of living, far removed from the habits of the rich.

4. From my great-grandfather,[5] not to have frequented public schools, and to have had good teachers at home, and to know that on such things a man should spend liberally.

5. From my governor, to be neither of the

---

[1] From the "Meditations." Translated by George Long.
[2] Annius Verus.
[3] His father's name also was Annius Verus.
[4] His mother was Domitia Calvilla, named also Lucilla.
[5] His mother's grandfather, Catilius Severus, may be referred to here.

MARCUS AURELIUS

green nor of the blue party at the games in the circus, nor a partizan either of the Parmularius or the Scutarius at the gladiators' fights; from him too I learned endurance of labor and to want little, and to work with my own hands, and not to meddle with other people's affairs, and not to be ready to listen to slander.

6. From Diognetus,[6] not to busy myself about trifling things, and not to give credit to what was said by miracle-workers and jugglers about incantations and the driving away of demons and such things; and not to breed quails [for fighting], not to give myself up passionately to such things; and to endure freedom of speech; and to have become intimate with philosophy; and to have been a hearer, first of Bacchius, then of Tandasis and Marcianus; and to have written dialogs in my youth; and to have desired a plank bed and skin, and whatever else of the kind belongs to the Grecian discipline.

7. From Rusticus[7] I received the impression that my character required improvement and discipline; and from him I learned not to be led astray to sophistic emulation, nor to writing on speculative matters, nor to delivering little hortatory orations, nor to showing myself off as a man who practises much discipline, or does benevolent

[6] The translator notes that, in the works of Justinus, is printed a letter from one Diognetus, a Gentile, who wished very much to know what the religion of the Christians was, and how it had taught them to believe neither in the gods of the Greeks nor the superstitions of the Jews. It has been suggested that this Diognetus may have been the tutor of Marcus Aurelius.

[7] Junius Rusticus, a Stoic philosopher, whom the author highly valued.

acts in order to make a display; and to abstain from rhetoric, and poetry, and fine writing; and not to walk about in the house in my outdoor dress, nor to do other things of the kind; and to write my letters with simplicity, like the letter which Rusticus wrote from Sinuessa to my mother; and with respect to those who have offended me by words, or done me wrong, to be easily disposed to be pacified and reconciled, as soon as they have shown a readiness to be reconciled; and to read carefully, and not to be satisfied with a superficial understanding of a book; not hastily to give my assent to those who talk overmuch; and I am indebted to him for being acquainted with the discourses of Epictetus.

8. From Apollonius[8] I learned freedom of will and undeviating steadiness of purpose; and to look to nothing else, not even for a moment, except to reason; and to be always the same, in sharp pains, on the occasion of the loss of a child, and in long illness; and to see clearly in a living example that the same man can be both most resolute and yielding, and not peevish in giving his instruction; and to have had before my eyes a man who clearly considered his experience and his skill in expounding philosophical principles as the smallest of his merits; and from him I learned how to receive from friends what are esteemed favors, without being either humbled by them or letting them pass unnoticed.

9. From Sextus,[9] a benevolent disposition, and the example of a family governed in a fatherly

[8] Apollonius of Chalcis, who came to Rome to be the author's preceptor. He was a rigid Stoic.

[9] Sextus of Chæronea, a grandson, or nephew, of Plutarch.

manner, and the idea of living conformably to nature; and gravity without affectation, and to look carefully after the interests of friends, and to tolerate ignorant persons and those who form opinions without consideration: he had the power of readily accommodating himself to all, so that intercourse with him was more agreeable than any flattery; and at the same time he was most highly venerated by those who associated with him; and he had the faculty both of discovering and ordering, in an intelligent methodical way, the principles necessary for life; and he never showed anger or any other passion, but was entirely free from passion, and also most affectionate; and he could express approbation without noisy display, and he possessed much knowledge without ostentation.

10. From Alexander[10] the grammarian, to refrain from fault-finding, and not in a reproachful way to chide those who uttered any barbarous or solecistic or strange-sounding expression; but dexterously to introduce the very expression which ought to have been used, and in the way of answer or giving confirmation, or joining in an inquiry about the thing itself, not about the word, or by some other fit suggestion.

11. From Fronto[11] I learned to observe what envy, and duplicity, and hypocrisy are in a tyrant, and that generally those among us who are called Patricians are rather deficient in paternal affection.

[10] Alexander, a native of Phrygia, wrote a commentary on Homer.

[11] Cornelius Fronto, a rhetorician and friend of the author.

he had overcome all passion for boys; and he considered himself no more than any other citizen; and he released his friends from all obligation to sup with him or to attend him of necessity when he went abroad, and those who had failed to accompany him, by reason of any urgent circumstances, always found him the same. I observed too his habit of careful inquiry in all matters of deliberation, and his persistency, and that he never stopt his investigation through being satisfied with appearances which first present themselves; and that his disposition was to keep his friends, and not to be soon tired of them, nor yet to be extravagant in his affection; and to be satisfied on all occasions, and cheerful; and to foresee things a long way off, and to provide for the smallest without display; and to check immediately popular applause and all flattery; and to be ever watchful over the things which were necessary for the administration of the empire, and to be a good manager of the expenditure, and patiently to endure the blame which he got for such conduct; and he was neither superstitious with respect to the gods, nor did he court men by gifts or by trying to please them, or by flattering the populace; but he showed sobriety in all things and firmness, and never any mean thoughts or action, nor love of novelty. . . .

17. To the gods I am indebted for having good grandfathers, good parents, a good sister, good teachers, good associates, good kinsmen and friends, nearly everything good. Further, I owe it to the gods that I was not hurried into any offense against any of them, tho I had a dis-

MARCUS AURELIUS

position which, if opportunity had offered, might have led me to do something of this kind; but, through their favor, there never was such a concurrence of circumstances as put me to the trial. Further, I am thankful to the gods that I was not longer brought up with my grandfather's concubine, and that I preserved the flower of my youth, and that I did not make proof of my virility before the proper season, but even deferred the time; that I was subjected to a ruler and a father who was able to take away all pride from me, and to bring me to the knowledge that it is possible for a man to live in a palace without wanting either guards or embroidered dresses, or torches and statues, and such-like show; but that it is in such a man's power to bring himself very near to the fashion of a private person, without being for this reason either meaner in thought, or more remiss in action, with respect to the things which must be done for the public interest in a manner that befits a ruler. I thank the gods for giving me such a brother,[15] who was able by his moral character to rouse me to vigilance over myself, and who, at the same time, pleased me by his respect and affection; that my children have not been stupid nor deformed in body; that I did not make more proficiency in rhetoric, poetry, and the other studies, in which I should perhaps have been completely engaged, if I had seen that I was making progress in them; that I made haste to place those who brought me up in the station of honor, which they seemed to desire, without

[15] His brother by adoption, L. Verus, is probably referred to here.

putting them off with hope of my doing it some time after, because they were then still young; that I knew Apollonius, Rusticus, Maximus; that I received clear and frequent impressions about living according to nature, and what kind of a life that is, so that, so far as depended on the gods, and their gifts, and help, and inspirations, nothing hindered me from forthwith living according to nature, tho I still fall short of it through my own fault, and through not observing the admonitions of the gods, and I may almost say, their direct instructions; that my body has held out so long in such a kind of life; that I never touched either Benedicta or Theodotus, and that, after having fallen into amatory passions, I was cured; and, tho I was often out of humor with Rusticus, I never did anything of which I had occasion to repent; that, tho it was my mother's fate to die young, she spent the last years of her life with me; that, whenever I wished to help any man in his need, or on any other occasion, I was never told that I had not the means of doing it; and that to myself the same necessity never happened, to receive anything from another; that I have such a wife, so obedient, and so affectionate, and so simple; that I had abundance of good masters for my children; and that remedies have been shown to me by dreams, both others, and against blood-spitting and giddiness; and that, when I had an inclination to philosophy, I did not fall into the hands of any sophist.

END OF VOLUME II.